DAILY SPARK

DAILY SPARK

366 QUOTES TO
GUIDE YOUR HEART,
MIND, AND SOUL

CURATED BY
DR. SARA BAKHTARY

DESIGNED BY
GIOVANNI DUBOIS

Spark & Sage Press

Copyright © 2025 Spark & Sage Press

All rights reserved. No part of this book may be reproduced, distributed, or transmitted in any form or by any means, including photocopying, recording, or other electronic or mechanical methods, without the prior written permission of the publisher, except in the case of brief quotations embodied in reviews, articles, and other noncommercial uses permitted by copyright law.

Every effort has been made to identify, credit, and accurately reproduce the quotations included in this book. Any errors or omissions are unintentional. The publisher and author assume no responsibility for errors, inaccuracies, or interpretations of the material contained herein. This book is intended for inspirational purposes only and should not be considered professional advice.

Quotations included in this book are drawn from a variety of sources in the public domain or are reproduced under fair use for purposes of commentary, education, or inspiration. Every effort has been made to ensure proper attribution. If you believe material has been used in error, please contact the publisher so that corrections can be made in subsequent editions.

For permission requests, write to:

Spark & Sage Press
Carlsbad, CA
sparkandsagepress@gmail.com

ISBN: 979-8-9932872-0-1 (Paperback)
ISBN: 979-8-9932872-1-8 (Hardcover)
ISBN: 979-8-9932872-2-5 (eBook)

Cover and interior design by Giovanni Dubois

Printed in the United States of America

To L & A, with love.

The Story Behind the Sparks

This book began as a labor of love, created as a guide and keepsake for my daughters. Within these pages are 366 quotes that have stayed with me over the years. They are words of encouragement, wisdom, and perspective from voices that have inspired and guided me. These quotes have lifted me in moments of doubt, offered clarity when I needed direction, and reminded me of the beauty and complexity of being human.

Growing up, I spent countless hours in my mom's hair salon, listening quietly as her clients shared their lives. They talked about love, loss, motherhood, heartbreak, and finding their way. I didn't know it then, but I was learning how much power lives in a single story and how deeply we can be shaped by the experiences of others. Those moments taught me that every person has something valuable to share, and every story holds a lesson worth learning.

In college, when I fell in love with my husband, one of the first gifts I gave him was a handful of handwritten quotes hidden all over his dorm room. They were small slips of paper, but each one carried something meaningful to me. A phrase or idea that helped me see the world with more hope or reminded me of the kind of person I wanted to be.

Quotes have a unique ability to distill profound truths into a few words, and this magic has captivated me ever since. I've always been drawn to the way a good quote can capture something so big in just a few words. That spark of insight, that shift in perspective, has a way of staying with you long after the words are gone.

My hope is that this book becomes a gentle companion in your life. You don't need to read it front to back. You can open it to today's date or flip to a random page when you need a little encouragement. Some quotes may resonate right away. Others might not, and that's okay. You will find what you need when you need it.

Let this book remind you that wisdom is all around us. It lives in books, in strangers, in conversations with friends. It is passed down, shared, forgotten, and rediscovered again. And every once in a while, it arrives at just the right time.

With love,
Sara Bakhtary

RELATIONSHIPS   COURAGE   GRATITUDE

WELL-BEING   KINDNESS   MOTIVATION

WISDOM

JANUARY

January 1

"Dreams come to tell us something about our lives that we are missing."

James Redfield

Writer, Screenwriter, and Film Producer, Best Known for *The Celestine Prophecy*

Dreams often reveal hidden desires, fears, or aspects of ourselves that we may be overlooking. Pay attention to your dreams, as they can offer valuable insights into your subconscious and guide you towards a more fulfilling life.

WISDOM

January 2

"And, when you want something, all the universe conspires in helping you to achieve it."

Paulo Coelho

Brazilian Lyricist and Novelist,
Best Known for International Bestseller *The Alchemist*

When you truly desire something and align your thoughts and actions with that desire, the universe seems to conspire to help you achieve it. Believe in your dreams, take inspired action, and watch as opportunities unfold.

WELL-BEING

January 3

"Don't worry about failures, worry about the chances you miss when you don't even try."

Jack Canfield

Author and Motivational Speaker,
Best Known for *Chicken Soup for the Soul*

Failing isn't the real fear—missing out on opportunities because you didn't try is. Taking a chance is always better than wondering "what if."

MOTIVATION

January 4

"Everyone enjoys being acknowledged and appreciated. Sometimes even the simplest act of gratitude can change someone's entire day. Take the time to recognize and value the people around you and appreciate those who make a difference in your lives."

Roy T. Bennett

Author, Best Known for *The Light in the Heart*

A little recognition can make a huge difference in someone's day. Show your appreciation, and watch how it lifts others up.

GRATITUDE

January 5

"Tell me and I'll forget; show me and I may remember; involve me and I'll understand."

Chinese Proverb

Active participation is the key to really learning something. Being hands-on sticks with you longer than just hearing or seeing it.

WISDOM

January 6

"Your body hears everything your mind says."

Naomi Judd

Country Music Singer, Songwriter, Actress, and Grammy Award Winner

If you're constantly thinking negative thoughts, your body will start feeling it too. Be kind to yourself in your mind because it affects everything else.

WELL-BEING

January 7

"If you want to fly, give up everything that weighs you down."

Attributed to Toni Morrison

Novelist and Nobel Prize Winner in Literature, Best Known for *Beloved*

Growth often requires release. The fears, doubts, and old stories we cling to can quietly anchor us in place. True success often means letting go—of fear, perfection, or old stories that no longer serve you. Lighten your load and rise.

MOTIVATION

January 8

"There are three things that grow more precious with age; old wood to burn, old books to read, and old friends to enjoy."

Henry W. Beecher

American Clergyman and Social Reformer

As you grow older, certain things become even more valuable: the warmth of a fire, the wisdom found in books, and the companionship of lifelong friends. Nurture these treasures and appreciate their enduring value.

RELATIONSHIPS

January 9

"If you're reading this...Congratulations, you're alive. If that's not something to smile about, then I don't know what is."

Chad Sugg

Singer, Songwriter, and Writer

Celebrate the gift of life and find joy in the simple fact that you're alive. Embrace each day with gratitude and enthusiasm, and make the most of every opportunity.

GRATITUDE

January 10

"Be kind whenever possible. It is always possible."

14th Dalai Lama

Spiritual Leader of Tibetan Buddhism,
Nobel Peace Prize Winner

Kindness is a choice, and it's always within your reach. Make a conscious effort to be kind to yourself and others, even in small ways. Your kindness can brighten someone's day and make the world a more compassionate place.

KINDNESS

January 11

"Yesterday I was clever, so I wanted to change the world. Today I am wise, so I am changing myself."

Rumi

(Jalal al-Din Rumi), Persian Poet and Sufi Mystic of the 13th Century

True wisdom comes with the recognition that there's always more to learn and understand. Embrace humility, be open to new perspectives, and focus on personal growth and self-improvement.

WISDOM

January 12

"Don't look at your feet to see if you are doing it right. Just dance."

Anne Lamott

Novelist, Nonfiction Writer, and Writing Teacher

Don't overthink or worry about perfection. Just let go, have fun, and express yourself freely. Embrace the joy of the moment and dance like nobody's watching.

WELL-BEING

January 13

"All our dreams can come true, if we have the courage to pursue them."

Walt Disney

Animator, Film Producer, Entrepreneur, and Founder of The Walt Disney Company

If you can imagine it, you can achieve it. Dreams are the seeds of possibility. Nurture your dreams, believe in their potential, and take action to turn them into reality.

MOTIVATION

January 14

"There is nothing on this earth more to be prized than true friendship."

Thomas Aquinas

Italian Theologian and Philosopher of the 13th Century

True friendship is one of life's greatest treasures. Nothing compares to the love and support of a real friend.

RELATIONSHIPS

January 15

"Live life with no excuses, travel with no regret."

Unknown

Live life to the fullest, without regrets or excuses. Embrace opportunities for adventure and travel, and don't let fear or hesitation hold you back from experiencing the world.

COURAGE

January 16

"If you want to achieve your goals, help others achieve theirs."

Zig Ziglar

Author, Salesman, and Motivational Speaker

Success is about lifting others up along the way. By helping others reach their dreams, you'll find your own success too.

KINDNESS

January 17

"You've gotta dance like there's nobody watching, love like you'll never be hurt, sing like there's nobody listening, and live like it's heaven on earth."

William W. Purkey

Educator and Professor of Counselor Education

Live life with abandon, expressing yourself freely and authentically. Dance, love, sing, and embrace every moment as if it were your last. Let go of inhibitions and live a life filled with joy and passion.

GRATITUDE

January 18

> "Very little is needed to make a happy life; it is all within yourself, in your way of thinking."

Marcus Aurelius

2nd Century Roman Emperor and Stoic Philosopher, Best Known for *Meditations*

Happiness doesn't require grand gestures or material possessions. It's a state of mind cultivated through gratitude, contentment, and a positive outlook on life.

WISDOM

January 19

"The secret of getting ahead is getting started."

Mark Twain

Author and Humorist,
Best Known for *The Adventures of Huckleberry Finn*

To make progress, you must begin. Taking the first step is the key to moving forward. Action breeds momentum, and momentum leads to progress.

MOTIVATION

January 20

"Yesterday is gone. Tomorrow has not yet come. We have only today. Let us begin."

Mother Teresa

Catholic Nun, Founder of the Missionaries of Charity, Nobel Peace Prize Winner

The past is behind you and the future is uncertain. Focus on today, because that's where life is happening right now.

WELL-BEING

January 21

"There are only two ways to live your life. One is as though nothing is a miracle. The other is as though everything is a miracle."

Attributed to Albert Einstein

Theoretical Physicist, Developer of the Theory of Relativity, Nobel Prize Winner in Physics

You have two choices in life: to see the world as ordinary and mundane or to recognize the magic and wonder in everything around you. Choose to embrace the extraordinary and find beauty in the everyday.

GRATITUDE

January 22

"You can't stay mad at somebody who makes you laugh."

Jay Leno

Comedian and Television Host,
Best Known for *The Tonight Show*

Laughter has a way of melting away anger and resentment. Choose forgiveness and understanding, especially with those who bring joy and laughter into your life.

RELATIONSHIPS

January 23

> "Miracles start to happen when you give as much energy to your dreams as you do to your fears."

Richard Wilkins
Motivational Speaker and Author

When you focus more on your dreams than your worries, amazing things start to unfold. Energy goes where attention flows.

COURAGE

January 24

"When I was young, I admired clever people. Now that I am old, I admire kind people."

Abraham Joshua Heschel

Rabbi, Jewish Theologian and Philosopher of the 20th Century

With age comes the realization that kindness is more important than being clever. Kindness is what really makes a lasting impact.

KINDNESS

January 25

"In nature, nothing is perfect and everything is perfect. Trees can be contorted, bent in weird ways, and they're still beautiful."

Alice Walker

Author, Poet, Activist, and Pulitzer Prize Winner, Best Known for *The Color Purple*

Nature embraces imperfection, and it's what makes it beautiful. There's beauty in being perfectly imperfect.

GRATITUDE

January 26

"When the power of love overcomes the love of power, the world will know peace."

Attributed to Jimi Hendrix

Rock Guitarist, Singer, and Songwriter

Lasting peace comes when love leads instead of power. It's a reminder that strength isn't about control or dominance, but about compassion and understanding. When love guides our choices, harmony follows.

WISDOM

January 27

"Do not take life too seriously. You will never get out of it alive."

Elbert Hubbard
Writer, Publisher, Artist, and Philosopher

Life is short, so don't stress about it too much. Enjoy the ride, laugh more, and let go of the little things.

WELL-BEING

January 28

"Whatever you do, always give 100% — unless you're donating blood."

Bill Murray

American Actor and Comedian

Give your all in everything you do, but know when it's time to hold back—like in funny or extreme situations! It's a reminder to work hard, but with a sense of humor.

MOTIVATION

January 29

"To travel is to take a journey into yourself."

Danny Kaye
Actor, Comedian, Singer, and Humanitarian

Traveling is more than just seeing new places—it's about discovering new parts of yourself. Every journey teaches you something.

COURAGE

January 30

"Friends are the family we choose for ourselves."

Edna Buchanan

Journalist, Crime Writer, and Pulitzer Prize Winner

Family is not only defined by blood. True friends are the people you choose to stand beside you, offering love, loyalty, and support just like family.

RELATIONSHIPS

January 31

"I've learned that people will forget what you said, people will forget what you did, but people will never forget how you made them feel."

Maya Angelou
American Poet, Author, and Civil Rights Activist

What sticks with people isn't your words or actions—it's the emotions you leave them with. Be mindful of the impact you have on other people's feelings.

KINDNESS

FEBRUARY

February 1

> "My mama always said, life is like a box of chocolates. You never know what you're gonna get."

Forrest Gump

Fictional Character from the Movie *Forrest Gump*, Played by Tom Hanks

Life is unpredictable, and that's part of what makes it interesting. Embrace the unknown with curiosity and an open mind.

WISDOM

February 2

"To be yourself in a world that is constantly trying to make you something else is the greatest accomplishment."

Ralph Waldo Emerson

Essayist, Poet, Philosopher, and
Leader of the Transcendentalist Movement

In a world where everyone tries to tell you how to live, staying true to who you are is a huge win. Authenticity is your superpower.

WELL-BEING

February 3

> "A life spent making mistakes is not only more honorable, but more useful than a life spent doing nothing."

George Bernard Shaw
Irish Playwright, Political Activist,
Academy Award Winner, and Nobel Prize Winner in Literature

Making mistakes is part of living fully and learning. A life without mistakes means you never took risks or tried anything new.

MOTIVATION

February 4

> "When we strive to become better than we are, everything around us becomes better too."

Paulo Coelho

Brazilian Lyricist and Novelist,
Best Known for International Bestseller *The Alchemist*

Personal growth and self-improvement have a ripple effect on your surroundings. When you strive to be your best self, you inspire others and contribute to a more positive and uplifting environment.

COURAGE

February 5

"Travelling - it leaves you speechless, then turns you into a storyteller."

Ibn Battuta

14th Century Moroccan Explorer and Scholar

Travel broadens your horizons and opens your eyes to new perspectives. It can leave you speechless with awe and wonder, and then inspire you to share your stories and experiences with others.

WISDOM

February 6

"If you truly love nature, you will find beauty everywhere."

Vincent van Gogh

Dutch Post-Impressionist Painter

When you appreciate nature, you see beauty in every part of it. Nature's wonders are all around, if you take the time to notice.

GRATITUDE

February 7

"Attention is the rarest and purest form of generosity."

Simone Weil

French Philosopher

True generosity is not about giving things. It is about giving your full presence. When you pay attention to someone, you offer them respect, validation, and care in a way that words or gifts alone cannot.

RELATIONSHIPS

February 8

"A winner is a dreamer who never gives up."

Nelson Mandela

South African Anti-Apartheid Activist,
Former President of South Africa, Nobel Peace Prize Winner

Success isn't about never failing; it's about refusing to quit. Keep chasing your dreams, no matter how tough it gets.

COURAGE

February 9

"A warm smile is the universal language of kindness."

William Arthur Ward

Motivational Writer and Columnist

A smile is understood everywhere as a sign of kindness and goodwill. It's a simple way to spread warmth.

KINDNESS

February 10

"Life is really simple, but we insist on making it complicated."

Confucius

Chinese Philosopher and Teacher,
Founder of Confucianism, 6th–5th Centuries BCE

Life is meant to be enjoyed, not overcomplicated. Find beauty in simplicity and let go of unnecessary stress and worries.

WISDOM

February 11

"The best bridge between despair and hope is a good night's sleep."

E. Joseph Cossman
Entrepreneur and Businessman

A good night's sleep can work wonders for your mental and emotional well-being. When you're feeling overwhelmed or discouraged, rest and recharge. A refreshed mind and body can help you find hope and clarity even in the darkest of times.

WELL-BEING

February 12

"Often when you think you're at the end of something, you're at the beginning of something else."

Fred Rogers

Children's Television Host, Author, and Minister, Best Known for *Mister Rogers' Neighborhood*

Endings are often just the start of new opportunities. What feels like the end might be the beginning of something great.

MOTIVATION

February 13

"In every walk with nature, one receives far more than he seeks."

John Muir

Naturalist, Writer, Conservationist, and
Advocate for Wilderness Preservation

Nature offers a wealth of wisdom and tranquility. Spend time outdoors, observe the natural world, and learn from its rhythms and cycles. Nature can teach you patience, resilience, and the importance of living in harmony with the environment.

GRATITUDE

February 14

"We're all a little weird. And life's a little weird. And when we find someone whose weirdness is compatible with ours, we join up with them and fall in mutual weirdness and call it love—true love."

Robert Fulghum

Author and Minister,
Best Known for *All I Really Need to Know I Learned in Kindergarten*

Love is about finding someone who embraces your quirks. When two people's "weirdness" matches, that's where real love happens.

RELATIONSHIPS

February 15

"Listen to the wind, it talks. Listen to the silence, it speaks. Listen to your heart, it knows."

Unknown

Pay attention to the quiet moments—they often carry the most wisdom. Your inner voice has the answers, if you just take the time to listen.

COURAGE

February 16

"Love is the bridge between you and everything."

Rumi

(Jalal al-Din Rumi), Persian Poet and
Sufi Mystic of the 13th Century

Love is the universal language, connecting us to each other, to the world around us, and to our own deeper selves. It allows us to build meaningful relationships, empathize with others, and find beauty in every corner of existence.

KINDNESS

February 17

"The only true wisdom is in knowing you know nothing."

Attributed to Socrates

Ancient Greek Philosopher,
Founder of the Socratic Method, 5th Century BCE

True wisdom lies in recognizing the vastness of knowledge and the limitations of our own understanding. Embrace a lifelong journey of learning and remain open to new perspectives and ideas.

WISDOM

February 18

> "Motivation comes from working on things we care about. It also comes from working with people we care about."

Sheryl Sandberg
Technology Executive, Writer, and Advocate for Women Leaders in the Workplace

True motivation stems from a sense of purpose and connection. Find work that aligns with your values and passions, and surround yourself with people who inspire and uplift you.

MOTIVATION

February 19

> "Take the attitude of a student, never be too big to ask questions, never know too much to learn something new."

Og Mandino

Author and Motivational Speaker,
Best Known for *The Greatest Salesman in the World*

Maintain a curious and open mind, always eager to learn and grow. Don't let ego or pride prevent you from seeking knowledge and asking questions. Embrace a lifelong journey of learning and discovery.

COURAGE

February 20

> "Love yourself first and everything else falls into line."

Lucille Ball

Actress, Comedian, Producer, and Studio Executive, Best Known for *I Love Lucy*

Self-love is the foundation for everything else in life. When you truly believe in yourself, everything else will start to fall into place.

WELL-BEING

February 21

"The most basic and powerful way to connect to another person is to listen. Just listen."

Rachel Naomi Remen

Physician, Clinical Professor, and Author of *Kitchen Table Wisdom*

Truly listening to someone can make a huge impact. It's one of the most valuable gifts you can give.

RELATIONSHIPS

February 22

"Believe you can, and you're halfway there."

Theodore Roosevelt

26th President of the United States, Writer, and Naturalist

Self-belief is the foundation of achievement. When you trust in your abilities and have confidence in your dreams, you unleash a powerful force within that propels you towards success. So embrace your potential and chase your aspirations with unwavering determination.

MOTIVATION

February 23

"Life is either a daring adventure or nothing at all."

Helen Keller

Author, Activist, and
Advocate for People with Disabilities

Life is meant to be lived boldly and passionately. Embrace adventure, take risks, and pursue your dreams with unwavering enthusiasm. Don't settle for a life of mediocrity; create a life that's extraordinary.

COURAGE

February 24

"Gratitude is the memory of the heart."

Jean Massieu

Deaf Educator and Pioneer in the
Development of French Sign Language

Gratitude isn't just a feeling—it's something you hold onto deep within your heart. It's a way of remembering the good in life.

GRATITUDE

February 25

"What wisdom can you find that is greater than kindness?"

Jean-Jacques Rousseau

Philosopher, Writer, and Composer of the 18th Century

True wisdom lies in being kind. It's the most important lesson anyone can learn.

KINDNESS

February 26

> "Travel changes you. As you move through this life and this world you change things slightly, you leave marks behind, however small. And in return, life — and travel — leaves marks on you."

Anthony Bourdain

Chef, Author, and Travel Documentarian

Travel changes you and shapes who you are. As you explore, you leave your mark and the world leaves its mark on you.

WISDOM

February 27

"Movement is the song of the body."

Vanda Scaravelli
Yoga Teacher and Author

Movement is a natural way for the body to express itself and come alive. Like a song reflects emotion, movement shows the body's rhythm and vitality.

WELL-BEING

February 28

"I never dreamed about success. I worked for it."

Estée Lauder
American Businesswoman and Cosmetics Entrepreneur

Success doesn't just happen because you want it—you've got to put in the effort. Dream big, but don't forget to hustle.

MOTIVATION

February 29

"You can choose courage, or you can choose comfort, but you cannot choose both."

Brené Brown

Research Professor, Author, and Podcast Host,
Best Known for Her Work on Vulnerability

Growth happens when you step outside your comfort zone. To be courageous, you have to leave behind what's familiar.

COURAGE

MARCH

March 1

"Relax. No one else knows what they're doing either."

Ricky Gervais

English Comedian, Actor, and Writer, Best Known for *The Office*

Don't worry—everyone is figuring things out as they go. You're not alone in feeling uncertain about life.

WISDOM

March 2

"Just one small positive thought in the morning can change your whole day."

14th Dalai Lama

Spiritual Leader of Tibetan Buddhism,
Nobel Peace Prize Winner

A single positive thought can set the tone for your entire day. Start each morning with gratitude, optimism, and a focus on the good. This simple practice can transform your outlook and attract more positivity into your life.

WELL-BEING

March 3

"If you don't like the road you're walking, start paving another one."

Dolly Parton

Singer-Songwriter and Philanthropist,
Best Known as the "Queen of Country Music"

If you're unhappy with your current path, don't be afraid to forge a new one. Take control of your life, make bold choices, and create a path that aligns with your values and aspirations.

MOTIVATION

March 4

"At the end of the day we can endure much more than we think we can."

Frida Kahlo

Mexican Painter,
Best Known for Her Self-Portraits and Symbolism

We often possess hidden reserves of strength and resilience. When faced with challenges, tap into your inner power and discover your capacity to overcome adversity.

COURAGE

March 5

> "There are two ways of spreading light: to be the candle or the mirror that reflects it."

Edith Wharton
Writer and Designer, Pulitzer Prize Winner

You have the power to illuminate the world, either by being a source of light yourself or by reflecting the light of others. Choose to inspire and uplift those around you through your own actions or by amplifying the goodness you see in the world.

KINDNESS

March 6

The way to a more productive, more inspired, more joyful life is getting enough sleep.

Arianna Huffington

Greek-American Author, Columnist, and Businesswoman, Best Known for *The Huffington Post*

Getting enough rest isn't a luxury, it's a necessity for a good life. Your body and mind need it to stay sharp, happy, and ready to take on the world.

WELL-BEING

March 7

"No matter who you are, no matter what you did, no matter where you've come from, you can always change, become a better version of yourself."

Madonna

American Singer, Songwriter, and Grammy Award Winner, Best Known as the "Queen of Pop"

Your past doesn't define you—you can always choose to grow and improve. It's never too late to become the best version of yourself.

MOTIVATION

March 8

> "Lots of people want to ride with you in the limo, but what you want is someone who will take the bus with you when the limo breaks down."

Oprah Winfrey
Talk Show Host, Actress, and Philanthropist

True friendship reveals itself when life isn't easy. The friends who stay close in difficult moments are the ones who really care. Real friendships thrive when they're tested.

RELATIONSHIPS

March 9

"Acknowledging the good that you already have in your life is the foundation for all abundance."

Eckhart Tolle

Spiritual Teacher and Author,
Best Known for *The Power of Now*

Gratitude shifts your focus from what is missing to what is present. By training your mind to recognize what is good, you open the door to more joy, peace, and abundance.

GRATITUDE

March 10

"Remember that the happiest people are not those getting more, but those giving more."

H. Jackson Brown Jr.

Author, Best Known for *Life's Little Instruction Book*

True happiness comes from generosity, not accumulation. Giving to others brings more joy than receiving.

KINDNESS

March 11

"Success is not the key to happiness. Happiness is the key to success. If you love what you are doing, you will be successful."

Albert Schweitzer
Theologian, Philosopher, Physician, Humanitarian, and Nobel Peace Prize Winner

True success isn't solely measured by external achievements, but by the joy and fulfillment you find in your pursuits. Passion fuels purpose, and when you're passionate about what you do, success naturally follows.

WISDOM

March 12

"Don't let yesterday take up too much of today."

Will Rogers

American Cowboy, Humorist, and Social Commentator

Don't let past mistakes or regrets consume your present. Learn from yesterday, but don't dwell on it. Focus on creating a better today and a brighter future.

WELL-BEING

March 13

"Where there's hope, there's life. It fills us with fresh courage and makes us strong again."

Anne Frank

Jewish Diarist and Holocaust Victim,
Best Known for *The Diary of a Young Girl*

Hope gives us the strength to keep going, even when things are hard. It's the fuel that keeps life moving forward.

MOTIVATION

March 14

> "You can't go back and change the beginning, but you can start where you are and change the ending."

Unknown

It's never too late to rewrite your story. Focus on where you're heading, not where you've been.

COURAGE

March 15

> "The quality of your life is the quality of your relationships."

Tony Robbins

Motivational Speaker, Life Coach, and Author

How happy and fulfilled you are depends on the people you surround yourself with. Strong relationships lead to a better life.

RELATIONSHIPS

March 16

"Listening is where love begins: listening to ourselves and then to our neighbors."

Fred Rogers

Children's Television Host, Author, and Minister,
Best Known for *Mister Rogers' Neighborhood*

Real love starts with truly listening to yourself and others. Being heard is the foundation of connection.

KINDNESS

March 17

"It's the everyday moments that bring the greatest joy."

Joanna Gaines

Interior Designer, Television Personality, and Entrepreneur, Best Known for *Fixer Upper*

Life's real beauty is in the small, everyday moments that often go unnoticed. These little things are what make life meaningful.

GRATITUDE

March 18

"From the ashes, I rose, and I stitched the pieces of my soul back together with gold."

Najwa Zebian

Lebanese–Canadian Activist, Author, Poet, and Speaker

Even after going through difficult times, you can rebuild yourself and become stronger. Your scars make you beautiful, like gold filling the cracks.

COURAGE

March 19

> "It is not the strongest of the species that survives, nor the most intelligent that survives. It is the one that is most adaptable to change."

Leon C. Megginson

Professor of Management and Marketing,
Paraphrasing Charles Darwin's Theory of Evolution

Survival and success aren't about being the biggest or smartest—they're about being able to adapt. Flexibility is what keeps you going when things change.

WISDOM

March 20

> "The secret to living well is eat half, walk double, laugh triple, and love without measure."

Tibetan proverb

A balanced life comes from moderation and lots of joy. Focus on enjoying simple pleasures like love, laughter, and health.

WELL-BEING

March 21

> "The best time to plant a tree was 20 years ago. The second best time is today."
>
> — Chinese Proverb

If you missed an opportunity before, don't dwell on it—start now.
It's never too late to take action.

MOTIVATION

March 22

> "I have learned over the years that when one's mind is made up, this diminishes fear; knowing what must be done does away with fear."

Rosa Parks

American Civil Rights Activist,
Best Known for Sparking the Montgomery Bus Boycott

When you have clarity and determination, fear diminishes. Make up your mind, commit to your goals, and take decisive action. This will empower you to overcome obstacles and achieve success.

COURAGE

March 23

> "Friendship is the golden thread that ties the heart of all the world."

John Evelyn

17th-Century English Writer, Diarist, and Gardener

Friendship is a universal bond that transcends borders and cultures. It's a source of shared experiences, mutual respect, and unconditional love. Nurture your friendships and build a strong support system that will carry you through life's journey.

RELATIONSHIPS

March 24

> "Being grateful does not mean that everything is necessarily good. It just means that you can accept it as a gift."

Roy T. Bennett

Author, Best Known for *The Light in the Heart*

Gratitude isn't about pretending everything is perfect—it's about appreciating the lessons and gifts in even the tough moments.

GRATITUDE

March 25

"What you do makes a difference, and you have to decide what kind of difference you want to make."

Jane Goodall

British Primatologist, Anthropologist, and Conservationist,
Best Known for Her Study of Chimpanzees

Every choice, big or small, leaves a mark on others and the world around us. When you act with compassion, you shape a legacy of goodness that continues long after the moment has passed.

KINDNESS

March 26

"Focus on the journey, not the destination. Joy is found not in finishing an activity but in doing it."

Greg Anderson

Author and Wellness Advocate

Happiness and growth come from being present in the process, not racing to the finish. Every step, even the challenging ones, shapes who you become. The journey, not the destination, is where you truly grow.

COURAGE

March 27

"Shoot for the moon. Even if you miss, you'll land among the stars."

Norman Vincent Peale

Minister and Author,
Best Known for *The Power of Positive Thinking*

Dream big—because even if you fall short, you'll still achieve more than you would have if you hadn't aimed high.

MOTIVATION

March 28

"To love oneself is the beginning of a lifelong romance."

Oscar Wilde
Irish Playwright, Poet, and Novelist

Self-love is the foundation for a fulfilling and joyful life. Embrace your strengths, accept your flaws, and treat yourself with kindness and compassion. Cultivate a loving relationship with yourself, and you'll attract positive experiences and healthy relationships into your life.

WELL-BEING

March 29

> "We can't control the direction of the wind, but we can adjust our sails."

Jimmy Dean
Country Music Singer, Television Host, and Entrepreneur

Life throws a lot of unexpected stuff our way, but you can always choose how you react to it. Flexibility is key to navigating challenges.

WISDOM

March 30

"Life is not what you alone make it. Life is the input of everyone who touched your life and every experience that entered it. We are all part of one another."

Yuri Kochiyama
Japanese-American Political and Human Rights Activist

Your life is shaped not only by your own actions but also by the people you encounter and the experiences you have. We are all interconnected, and our lives are enriched by the contributions of others.

RELATIONSHIPS

March 31

"Write it on your heart that every day is the best day in the year."

Ralph Waldo Emerson

Essayist, Poet, Philosopher, and
Leader of the Transcendentalist Movement

Start each day with the belief that it's going to be amazing. This mindset transforms your experience of life.

GRATITUDE

APRIL

April 1

"Our greatest glory is not in never falling, but in rising every time we fall."

Attributed to Confucius

Chinese Philosopher and Teacher,
Founder of Confucianism, 6th–5th Centuries BCE

True strength lies not in avoiding failure, but in the ability to rise above it. Embrace setbacks as learning opportunities and use them to fuel your resilience and determination.

COURAGE

April 2

"He who lives in harmony with himself lives in harmony with the universe."

Marcus Aurelius

2nd Century Roman Emperor and Stoic Philosopher, Best Known for *Meditations*

When you're at peace with yourself, everything around you feels more aligned. Inner balance leads to outer peace.

WELL-BEING

April 3

"People don't take trips . . . trips take people."

John Steinbeck

American Writer and Nobel Prize Winner in Literature, Best Known for *The Grapes of Wrath*

When you travel, it's not just about the destination—it's about how the experience changes you. The journey shapes who you are.

MOTIVATION

April 4

"Travel is like an endless university. You never stop learning."

Harvey Lloyd

Photographer, Best Known for Realistic and Abstract Photography

Every place you visit teaches you something new. Traveling is one of the best ways to keep learning throughout life.

WISDOM

April 5

"Just don't give up trying to do what you really want to do. Where there is love and inspiration, I don't think you can go wrong."

Ella Fitzgerald

American Jazz and Swing Singer,
Grammy Award Winner, Best Known as the "First Lady of Song"

If you're passionate about something, keep going after it. As long as you're driven by love and inspiration, you're on the right path.

COURAGE

April 6

"There are always flowers for those who want to see them."

Henri Matisse

French Artist and Painter

Beauty and positivity are everywhere if you're willing to look for them. It's all about perspective and what you choose to notice.

GRATITUDE

April 7

"The difference between ordinary and extraordinary is that little extra."

Jimmy Johnson
American Football Coach and Two-Time Super Bowl Champion

Going the extra mile is what turns something good into something great. Small efforts can make a big difference.

MOTIVATION

April 8

"If you judge people, you have no time to love them."

Mother Teresa

Catholic Nun, Founder of the Missionaries of Charity,
Nobel Peace Prize Winner

Judgment creates barriers and prevents genuine connection. Choose to focus on love, understanding, and acceptance, rather than judging others based on your own limited perspective.

RELATIONSHIPS

April 9

> "Compassion brings us to a stop, and for a moment, we rise above ourselves."

Mason Cooley
Author and Professor of English

Compassion allows us to connect with others on a deeper level, transcending our own perspectives and experiences. Practice empathy and kindness, and strive to understand and support those around you.

KINDNESS

April 10

"You are the designer of your destiny; you are the author of your story."

Lisa Nichols

Motivational Speaker and Author

You are the architect of your own life. Take ownership of your choices, write your own story, and create a destiny that reflects your dreams and aspirations.

COURAGE

April 11

"There is no shame in not knowing; the shame lies in not finding out."

Russian proverb

It's okay not to know everything, but not being curious enough to learn is where the problem lies. Never stop seeking answers.

MOTIVATION

April 12

"Do the best you can. No one can do more than that."

John Wooden

Basketball Coach and Player, Won 10 NCAA National Championships as Head Coach of UCLA

Strive to do your best in every endeavor, but don't be afraid to make mistakes or fall short. Give your all, learn from your experiences, and keep moving forward.

WELL-BEING

April 13

"To be fully seen by somebody, then, and be loved anyhow—this is a human offering that can border on miraculous."

Elizabeth Gilbert

Author and Journalist, Best Known for *Eat, Pray, Love*

To be truly seen and accepted for who you are, flaws and all, and to be loved unconditionally, is a rare and precious gift. Embrace those who offer you this kind of love and cherish the connections that allow you to be your authentic self.

RELATIONSHIPS

April 14

> "The first to apologize is the bravest. The first to forgive is the strongest. The first to forget is the happiest."

Unknown

Owning up to mistakes takes courage, and letting go of grudges takes strength. True happiness comes from moving forward without carrying the past.

WISDOM

April 15

"We live in a wonderful world that is full of beauty, charm and adventure. There is no end to the adventures we can have if only we seek them with our eyes open."

Jawaharlal Nehru
Indian Independence Leader and First Prime Minister of India

The world is full of amazing things, but you need to be open to seeing them. Life is an adventure if you choose to see it that way.

GRATITUDE

April 16

"If we are asking for the world to be kind, we must first ask what are we doing to add more kindness to the world. If we are asking for the world to be more loving, we must first ask what are we doing to add more love to the world. We are the vessels for the things we seek."

Joél Leon

Performer, Author, and Storyteller

If you want more kindness and love in the world, start by being kind and loving yourself. Be the change you want to see.

KINDNESS

April 17

"Courage is not the absence of fear, but the triumph over it."

Nelson Mandela

South African Anti-Apartheid Activist,
Former President of South Africa, Nobel Peace Prize Winner

True courage isn't about being fearless — it's about embracing your fears and moving forward despite them. Stepping outside your comfort zone, chasing your dreams, and standing up for what's right, even when it feels daunting — that's the heart of true bravery.

COURAGE

April 18

"Vulnerability is the birthplace of innovation, creativity and change."

Brené Brown

Research Professor, Author, and Podcast Host,
Best Known for Her Work on Vulnerability

Being open and real, even when it's hard, leads to new ideas and growth. Vulnerability is where transformation starts.

WISDOM

April 19

"Don't say you don't have enough time. You have exactly the same number of hours per day that were given to Helen Keller, Pasteur, Michelangelo, Mother Teresa, Leonardo da Vinci, Thomas Jefferson, and Albert Einstein."

H. Jackson Brown Jr.

Author, Best Known for *Life's Little Instruction Book*

Time is a precious resource, and we all have the same 24 hours in a day. Don't make excuses about not having enough time; prioritize your goals and make conscious choices to invest your time wisely.

MOTIVATION

April 20

"Pray thankfulness for this Earth we are. For this becoming we are. For this sunlight touching skin we are. For the cooling of the dark we are."

Joy Harjo

Poet and Musician,
First U.S. Native American Poet Laureate

We are not separate from the Earth — we are part of it. Every breath, every ray of sun, every shift from day to night is a gift. Gratitude reminds us that life itself is sacred and that we belong to the whole.

GRATITUDE

April 21

> "Those who have a 'why' to live, can bear with almost any 'how.'"

Viktor E. Frankl

Austrian psychiatrist and Holocaust survivor, Best Known for *Man's Search for Meaning*

When you have a clear purpose or reason to keep going, you can endure almost anything. Purpose gives you strength.

WELL-BEING

April 22

"Success is falling nine times and getting up 10."

Jon Bon Jovi

Singer, Songwriter, and
Founder of the Rock Band Bon Jovi

Success is not about avoiding failure, but about persevering through it. Embrace challenges, learn from your mistakes, and keep getting back up, even when you fall.

COURAGE

April 23

"If you want to lift yourself up, lift up someone else."

Booker T. Washington
Educator, Author, Leader, and Advisor to U.S. Presidents

Helping others is one of the best ways to feel better about yourself. Lifting others up creates a positive cycle.

RELATIONSHIPS

April 24

"The best and most beautiful things in the world cannot be seen or even touched - they must be felt with the heart."

Helen Keller

Author, Activist, and
Advocate for People with Disabilities

The most meaningful experiences in life – love, joy, connection – can't be bought or seen. They're felt deep within your heart and soul.

GRATITUDE

April 25

"A single act of kindness throws out roots in all directions, and the roots spring up and make new trees."

Amelia Earhart

American Aviator, Record-Setting Pilot, and Advocate for Women in Aviation

One small kind act can create a ripple effect, spreading positivity far beyond what you can see. Every time we choose kindness, we help something new take root in the world.

KINDNESS

April 26

"Attitude is a choice.
Happiness is a choice.
Optimism is a choice.
Kindness is a choice.
Giving is a choice.
Respect is a choice.
Whatever choice you make
makes you. Choose wisely."

Roy T. Bennett

Author, Best Known for *The Light in the Heart*

Your attitude and actions shape who you are. Every day, you have the power to choose positivity, kindness, and happiness.

WISDOM

April 27

"You don't have to see the whole staircase, just take the first step."

Martin Luther King Jr.
Baptist Minister, Civil Rights Leader, and Nobel Peace Prize Winner

You don't need to know the whole plan—just start. The first step is always the hardest, but it gets you moving.

COURAGE

April 28

"One child, one teacher, one book, one pen can change the world."

Malala Yousafzai

Pakistani Activist for Girls' Education and Nobel Peace Prize Winner

Even the smallest actions can have a profound impact on the world. A single child, teacher, book, or pen can spark change, ignite inspiration, and transform lives. Never underestimate the power of your individual contribution.

MOTIVATION

April 29

"If your heart is broken, make art with the pieces."

Shane Koyczan
Spoken Word Poet and Storytelling Activist

Turn your pain into something beautiful. When you're broken, use your creativity to heal and grow.

WELL-BEING

April 30

"Treasure your relationships, not your possessions."

Anthony J. D'Angelo
Motivational Speaker and Author

The things you own can't bring you true happiness. It's the people in your life that make everything worthwhile.

RELATIONSHIPS

MAY

May 1

"Intelligence is the ability to adapt to change."

Stephen Hawking

British Theoretical Physicist, Cosmologist, and Author,
Advocate for People with Disabilities

Smart people aren't just book-smart—they know how to roll with the punches. Flexibility and adaptability are the marks of true intelligence.

May 2

"It's the possibility of having a dream come true that makes life interesting."

Paulo Coelho

Brazilian Lyricist and Novelist,
Best Known for International Bestseller *The Alchemist*

The possibility of achieving your dreams is what makes life exciting and meaningful. Embrace your aspirations, pursue your passions, and never give up on the things that make your heart sing.

MOTIVATION

May 3

"A day without laughter is a day wasted."

Charlie Chaplin

English Comic Actor and Filmmaker,
Best Known for His Silent Film Comedies

Laughter is the soundtrack to a happy and fulfilling life. Find humor in everyday moments, surround yourself with people who make you laugh, and don't take life too seriously.

WELL-BEING

May 4

"If you don't get out of the box you've been raised in, you won't understand how much bigger the world is."

Angelina Jolie

Actress and Humanitarian, Academy Award Winner

Break free from the limitations and expectations imposed on you by your upbringing or environment. Explore the world, embrace new experiences, and discover the vastness of possibilities that lie beyond your comfort zone.

COURAGE

May 5

"Peace comes within the souls of people when they realize their oneness with the universe."

Black Elk

19th–20th Century Oglala Lakota Holy Man

Peace begins when you remember your connection to everything around you. You are not separate from the world but part of its rhythm and balance. When you live with that awareness, a quiet harmony fills your heart.

WISDOM

May 6

> "Vision is not enough. It must be combined with venture. It is not enough to stare up the steps; we must also step up the stairs."

Václav Havel
Czech Writer, Playwright, Politician, and Former President of the Czech Republic

Dreams are great, but they need action to become reality. You can't just plan—you have to take real steps toward your goals.

MOTIVATION

May 7

"For every minute you are angry you lose sixty seconds of happiness."

Ralph Waldo Emerson

Essayist, Poet, Philosopher, and
Leader of the Transcendentalist Movement

Holding onto anger only robs you of joy. Let go of what's making you upset so you can make room for happiness.

WELL-BEING

May 8

> "We come to love not by finding a perfect person, but by learning to see an imperfect person perfectly."

Sam Keen

Philosopher, Author, and Professor

Real love isn't about perfection or appearances. It's about seeing someone fully — flaws, strengths, and all — and choosing to love them anyway. True connection grows from acceptance, not idealization.

RELATIONSHIPS

May 9

"The older you get, the more fragile you understand life to be. I think that's good motivation for getting out of bed joyfully each day."

Julia Roberts

American Actress and Academy Award Winner

As you age, you realize how precious and delicate life is, which makes each day even more special. Wake up with gratitude for the time you have.

GRATITUDE

May 10

"Act as if what you do makes a difference. It does."

William James
Psychologist and Philosopher of the Late 19th Century

Every action you take has an impact, even if it feels small. Believe that what you do matters, because it does.

KINDNESS

May 11

"We travel, initially, to lose ourselves; and we travel, next, to find ourselves."

Pico Iyer

Essayist and Travel Writer

Travel teaches you about yourself as much as the world around you. In losing your familiar patterns, you discover what truly matters. Every journey, near or far, becomes a path back to who you are.

WISDOM

May 12

"You have brains in your head. You have feet in your shoes. You can steer yourself any direction you choose. You're on your own. And you know what you know. And YOU are the one who'll decide where to go..."

Dr. Seuss

(Theodor Seuss Geisel),
American Children's Author and Illustrator

You have the intelligence, the resources, and the freedom to choose your own path in life. Trust your instincts, make informed decisions, and take responsibility for your journey.

WELL-BEING

May 13

"If you fail to plan, you plan to fail."

Attributed to Benjamin Franklin
American Polymath, Inventor, and Founding Father

Without a plan, you're setting yourself up for failure. Preparation is key to achieving your goals.

MOTIVATION

May 14

"If you want something you never had, you have to do something you've never done."

Unknown

To achieve new goals, you have to step out of your comfort zone. Trying something different is the first step to getting what you want.

COURAGE

May 15

> "Each friend represents a world in us, a world possibly not born until they arrive, and it is only by this meeting that a new world is born."

Anaïs Nin
20th-Century Diarist and Author

Every meaningful connection awakens something new within you. Each person you meet reveals a part of yourself you might never have discovered alone. Through friendship, your world quietly expands.

RELATIONSHIPS

May 16

"Do not spoil what you have by desiring what you have not; remember that what you now have was once among the things you only hoped for."

Epicurus

Ancient Greek Philosopher,
Founder of Epicureanism, 4th–3rd Century BCE

Being satisfied with what you have is the ultimate form of wealth. True richness comes from contentment, not from what you own.

GRATITUDE

May 17

> "In seeking happiness for others, you will find it in yourself."

Wayne Walter Dyer

Author and Motivational Speaker

Helping others find joy is the quickest way to find your own happiness. Kindness and generosity bring their own rewards.

KINDNESS

May 18

"It's not whether you get knocked down, it's whether you get up."

Vince Lombardi

American Football Coach and Executive

Resilience is key. It's not about avoiding setbacks, but about having the strength and determination to bounce back from them. Every time you get back up, you grow stronger and more capable.

COURAGE

May 19

"It takes courage to grow up and become who you really are."

E. E. Cummings

20th-Century Poet and Painter

Becoming yourself is one of life's deepest lessons. It asks you to listen to your heart, trust your truth, and grow beyond who you've been. Wisdom begins when you have the courage to be real.

WISDOM

May 20

"Before anything else, preparation is the key to success."

Alexander Graham Bell
Inventor, Scientist, and Engineer,
Best Known for Inventing the Telephone

Success starts with being prepared. The groundwork you lay today sets you up for success tomorrow.

MOTIVATION

May 21

> "Beauty is how you feel inside, and it reflects in your eyes. It is not something physical."

Sophia Loren
Italian Actress and Academy Award Winner

Real beauty radiates from within. When you nurture confidence and peace inside yourself, it naturally shines through. How you feel becomes the truest reflection of who you are.

WELL-BEING

May 22

"Life isn't about waiting for the storm to pass. It's about learning how to dance in the rain."

Vivian Greene

Artist, Author, and Entrepreneur

Don't wait for life to be perfect—learn to find joy in the middle of chaos. Embrace the challenges and find happiness despite them.

COURAGE

May 23

"There is always some madness in love. But there is also always some reason in madness."

Friedrich Nietzsche

19th-Century German Philosopher and Cultural Critic

Love is a complex and passionate emotion that can sometimes feel a bit crazy. But even in its intensity, there's a deeper logic and reason behind it. Embrace the passion and embrace the vulnerability that comes with love.

RELATIONSHIPS

May 24

> "Some people look for a beautiful place. Others make a place beautiful."

Hazrat Inayat Khan

Indian Sufi Musician and Pioneer of Sufism in the West

Beauty isn't always about finding the perfect setting—it's about creating beauty wherever you go. You have the power to make any place beautiful.

KINDNESS

May 25

> "When you are grateful, fear disappears and abundance appears."

Tony Robbins
Motivational Speaker, Life Coach, and Author

Focusing on gratitude can dissolve fear and open your life to abundance. Gratitude changes your mindset, which changes everything.

GRATITUDE

May 26

"No matter what people tell you, words and ideas can change the world."

Robin Williams

Actor, Comedian, and Academy Award Winner

Your words and ideas have the power to inspire, motivate, and create change. Don't underestimate the impact you can have on the world through your voice and your vision.

MOTIVATION

May 27

"It's your life; you don't need someone's permission to live the life you want. Be brave to live from your heart."

Roy T. Bennett

Author, Best Known for *The Light in the Heart*

Don't wait for anyone to give you the green light to chase your dreams. You're in control, so go after what you truly want.

WELL-BEING

May 28

"Be courageous. Challenge orthodoxy. Stand up for what you believe in. When you are in your rocking chair talking to your grandchildren many years from now, be sure you have a good story to tell."

Amal Clooney
British-Lebanese Lawyer and Human Rights Activist

Live a life of courage and conviction. Don't be afraid to challenge the status quo, question conventional wisdom, and stand up for what you believe in. Create a legacy that inspires future generations and leaves a positive mark on the world.

COURAGE

May 29

> "Real love is accepting other people the way they are without trying to change them."

Don Miguel Ruiz

Mexican Author and Toltec Spiritual Teacher, Best Known for *The Four Agreements*

True love involves accepting others for who they are, without trying to change or control them. Embrace their individuality, celebrate their strengths, and support them on their own journey.

RELATIONSHIPS

May 30

"We delight in the beauty of the butterfly, but rarely admit the changes it has gone through to achieve that beauty."

Maya Angelou

American Poet, Author, and Civil Rights Activist

Transformation and growth often involve challenges and discomfort. Embrace the process of change, even when it's difficult, and recognize that it's essential for reaching your full potential and achieving your dreams.

WISDOM

May 31

"Thousands of candles can be lighted from a single candle, and the life of the candle will not be shortened. Happiness never decreases by being shared."

Attributed to the Buddha

(Sidhartha Gautama),
Religious Teacher and Founder of Buddhism

Sharing happiness doesn't take it away from you—it multiplies it. The more you spread kindness and joy, the more it comes back to you.

KINDNESS

JUNE

June 1

"Fall down seven times, stand up eight."

Japanese Proverb

No matter how many times you fail, keep getting back up. Resilience is the key to success.

COURAGE

June 2

"Say something positive, and you'll see something positive."

Jim Thompson

Founder of the Positive Coaching Alliance,
Advocate for Positive Youth Sports

Your words and thoughts shape your reality. Focus on the good, and you'll start noticing more of it around you.

WELL-BEING

June 3

"The way to get started is to quit talking and begin doing."

Walt Disney

Animator, Film Producer, Entrepreneur, and Founder of The Walt Disney Company

Stop overthinking, stop talking about what you want to do, and just take that first step. Action is the key to making things happen.

MOTIVATION

June 4

"To learn a language is to have one more window from which to look at the world."

Chinese Proverb

Learning a new language opens doors to new cultures, perspectives, and opportunities. Embrace the challenge of language learning and expand your understanding of the world.

WISDOM

June 5

"The way I see it, if you want the rainbow, you gotta put up with the rain!"

Dolly Parton

Singer-Songwriter and Philanthropist,
Best Known as the "Queen of Country Music"

You can't have the good without going through some tough times. The challenges are what make the rewards so sweet.

COURAGE

June 6

"Follow your passion. Stay true to yourself. Never follow anyone else's path unless you're in the woods and you're lost and you see a path. Then, by all means, follow that path."

Ellen DeGeneres

Comedian, Talk Show Host, Actress, and Emmy Award Winner

Always pursue what feels right to you, but if you find yourself lost, don't hesitate to take help when it's there. It's a playful way to say, stay true but be practical.

WELL-BEING

June 7

"Great things are not done by impulse, but by a series of small things brought together."

Vincent van Gogh

Dutch Post-Impressionist Painter

Big achievements don't happen all at once. They're the result of many small, steady actions that add up over time. Every choice and effort, no matter how small, becomes part of something greater.

MOTIVATION

June 8

"It is better to be hated for what you are than to be loved for what you are not."

André Gide

French author and Nobel Prize winner in Literature

It is better to live truthfully than to chase approval. When you show up as your real self, not everyone will understand you, but the right people will. Authenticity creates deeper, lasting connections than pretending ever could.

RELATIONSHIPS

June 9

> "There is no way to happiness—happiness is the way."

Thích Nhất Hạnh

Vietnamese Buddhist Monk, Poet, and Peace Activist

Happiness isn't a destination you reach; it's a way of being and a mindset you cultivate along the way. Embrace the present moment, find joy in the journey, and choose happiness as your guiding principle.

WISDOM

June 10

"Once a year, go somewhere you have never been before."

Attributed to the 14th Dalai Lama

Spiritual Leader of Tibetan Buddhism,
Nobel Peace Prize Winner

Make it a habit to explore new places, even if it's just once a year. Experiencing something new can refresh your perspective on life.

COURAGE

June 11

"Knowing yourself is the beginning of all wisdom."

Attributed to Aristotle

Ancient Greek Philosopher and Polymath,
Student of Plato and Teacher of Alexander the Great,
4th Century BCE

True wisdom comes from understanding who you are. Once you know yourself, you can navigate life with clarity and purpose.

WELL-BEING

June 12

"Opportunities are like sunrises. If you wait too long, you miss them."

William Arthur Ward
Motivational Writer and Columnist

Opportunities are fleeting and often come unexpectedly. Be proactive, seize the moment, and don't let fear or hesitation hold you back. Embrace new experiences and chase your dreams with courage and determination.

MOTIVATION

June 13

"One does not fall in love; one grows into love, and love grows in him."

Karl Menninger
American Psychiatrist and Author

Love isn't a sudden event—it's something that deepens over time. It grows as you nurture it.

RELATIONSHIPS

June 14

"Travel is the only thing you can buy that makes you richer."

Unknown

Investing in travel is an investment in yourself. It provides experiences and memories that money can't buy, broadening your perspective and enriching your life in countless ways.

WISDOM

June 15

"Twenty years from now you will be more disappointed by the things that you didn't do than by the ones you did do."

H. Jackson Brown Jr.

Author, Best Known for *Life's Little Instruction Book*

Gratitude grows when you live boldly and savor each experience. Regret fades when you take chances and follow what calls to your heart. The memories made along the way become life's true treasures.

GRATITUDE

June 16

> "The meaning of life is to find your gift. The purpose of life is to give it away."

David S. Viscott
Psychiatrist, Author, and Radio Host

Your unique talents and gifts are meant to be shared with the world. Finding your purpose is about using those gifts to help others.

KINDNESS

June 17

"It's not always that we need to do more but rather that we need to focus on less."

Nathan W. Morris
Personal Finance Coach and Speaker

Sometimes the key to success is simplifying, not adding more. Narrowing your focus can lead to bigger results.

WELL-BEING

June 18

> "Happiness is not the absence of problems; it's the ability to deal with them."

Steve Maraboli
Motivational Speaker and Author

It's not about avoiding problems but learning how to handle them with grace. Happiness comes from resilience, not perfection.

WISDOM

June 19

"The world is a book, and those who do not travel read only a page."

Attributed to Saint Augustine

Theologian and Philosopher

The world is a vast and diverse place, full of wonders waiting to be discovered. Travel expands your horizons, broadens your perspective, and enriches your understanding of different cultures and ways of life.

MOTIVATION

June 20

"In the middle of difficulty lies opportunity."

Attributed to Albert Einstein

Theoretical Physicist, Developer of the Theory of Relativity, Nobel Prize Winner in Physics

Challenges and setbacks are inevitable, but within them lie hidden opportunities for growth and transformation. Embrace difficulties as chances to learn, adapt, and emerge stronger than before.

COURAGE

June 21

"Don't think or judge, just listen."

Sarah Dessen
Novelist, Best Known for Young Adult Fiction

Sometimes the most powerful communication comes from simply listening. Set aside your own judgments and opinions, and truly hear what others have to say. Active listening fosters understanding, empathy, and connection.

RELATIONSHIPS

June 22

"Happiness is not having what you want, but wanting what you have."

Hyman Schachtel

American Rabbi,
Best Known for Delivering Inaugural Prayer for
President Lyndon B. Johnson

True happiness comes from appreciating what you already have, not constantly chasing after more. Gratitude is the key to contentment.

GRATITUDE

June 23

"No act of kindness, no matter how small, is ever wasted."

Aesop

Ancient Greek Storyteller,
Lived Around 6th Century BCE

Every act of kindness, whether it's a simple gesture or a grand act of generosity, leaves a lasting positive impact. Spreading kindness not only brightens someone else's day but also nourishes your own soul and creates a chain reaction of compassion.

KINDNESS

June 24

"The universe is energy, energy that responds to our expectations."

James Redfield

Writer, Screenwriter, and Film Producer, Best Known for *The Celestine Prophecy*

What you expect from life often comes true because of the energy you put into it. Your thoughts shape your reality.

WISDOM

June 25

> "What matters in life is not what happens to you, but what you remember and how you remember it."

Gabriel García Márquez

Colombian Novelist and Nobel Prize Winner in Literature, Best Known for *One Hundred Years of Solitude*

It's not just the events of life that shape you—it's how you choose to remember them. Your perspective on the past influences your future.

WELL-BEING

June 26

"If you are not willing to learn, no one can help you. If you are determined to learn, no one can stop you."

Zig Ziglar
Author, Salesman, and Motivational Speaker

Your attitude towards learning determines your success. Be open to growth, and nothing will hold you back.

MOTIVATION

June 27

"Vulnerability sounds like truth and feels like courage. Truth and courage aren't always comfortable, but they're never weakness."

Brené Brown

Research Professor, Author, and Podcast Host,
Best Known for Her Work on Vulnerability

Being vulnerable is one of the bravest things you can do. It's uncomfortable, but it's where real strength lies.

COURAGE

June 28

"A life is not important except in the impact it has on other lives."

Jackie Robinson
American Baseball Player and Civil Rights Activist

Your life's value is measured by the difference you make in others' lives. Kindness, support, and love are your true legacy.

RELATIONSHIPS

June 29

"We do not remember days, we remember moments."

Cesare Pavese

Italian Novelist and Poet

Life's true beauty lives in the small, fleeting moments. When we pause to notice them, even ordinary days feel extraordinary.

GRATITUDE

June 30

"Carry out a random act of kindness, with no expectation of reward, safe in the knowledge that one day someone might do the same for you."

Diana, Princess of Wales

Member of the British Royal Family,
Mother of Princes William and Harry, Humanitarian

Do kind things without expecting anything in return. The kindness you give may come back to you in ways you don't expect.

KINDNESS

JULY

July 1

"Be curious. And however difficult life may seem, there is always something you can do and succeed at. It matters that you don't just give up."

Stephen Hawking

British Theoretical Physicist, Cosmologist, and Author, Advocate for People with Disabilities

Curiosity keeps the mind alive even when life feels hard. It opens doors to new ideas, new strength, and new possibilities. No matter your limits, there is always something meaningful you can do, and that effort itself gives life purpose.

WISDOM

July 2

> "You don't always need a plan. Sometimes you just need to breathe, trust, let go and see what happens."

Mandy Hale
Author, Blogger, and Motivational Speaker

Not everything in life requires a plan. Sometimes, the best things come when you let go and allow life to unfold naturally.

WELL-BEING

July 3

"There is nothing impossible to they who will try."

Attributed to Alexander the Great

King of Macedon and Military Leader, 4th Century BCE

If you're willing to put in the effort, nothing is out of reach. Determination can make the impossible possible.

MOTIVATION

July 4

"The hard days are what make you stronger."

Aly Raisman

American Gymnast and Olympic Gold Medalist

Challenges and tough times build resilience and inner strength. Embrace them as opportunities for growth and self-discovery.

COURAGE

July 5

> "By working faithfully eight hours a day, you may eventually get to be boss and work twelve hours a day."

Don Herold
Humorist and Writer

Hard work can lead to more responsibilities, but be careful what you wish for. Success often comes with added pressure.

WISDOM

July 6

"To me, if life boils down to one thing, it's movement. To live is to keep moving."

Jerry Seinfeld

American Stand-Up Comedian and Actor, Best Known for the Sitcom *Seinfeld*

Life is about constant growth and change. Keep moving forward, both physically and mentally, to fully experience it.

WELL-BEING

July 7

"Don't count the days, make the days count."

Muhammad Ali

Professional Boxer, Activist, and Philanthropist

Focus on making each day meaningful and purposeful, rather than simply counting the days. Live with intention, create lasting memories, and make the most of every moment.

MOTIVATION

July 8

"The only thing we have to fear is fear itself."

Franklin D. Roosevelt

*32nd President of the United States,
Led Through the Great Depression and World War II*

The greatest obstacle we face is often our own fear. Conquer your fears, embrace challenges, and step boldly into the unknown. Remember, courage is not the absence of fear, but the triumph over it.

COURAGE

July 9

"Live as if you were to die tomorrow. Learn as if you were to live forever."

Attributed to Mahatma Gandhi

Leading Figure of the Indian Independence Movement, Advocate for Nonviolent Resistance

Live each day to the fullest, appreciating every moment as if it were your last. At the same time, cultivate a thirst for knowledge and a lifelong commitment to learning and growth.

WISDOM

July 10

"Sometimes the most productive thing you can do is relax."

Mark Black

Heart and Double-Lung Transplant Recipient, 4-time Marathon Runner, and Author

Productivity is not only about constant effort. Pausing to rest and recharge often gives you the clarity and energy you need to move forward more effectively. Sometimes the wisest action is to simply slow down.

WELL-BEING

July 11

"The people who are crazy enough to think they can change the world are the ones who do."

Steve Jobs

Entrepreneur, Inventor, and Investor,
Co-Founder of Apple

It's the bold thinkers, the dreamers, who actually make the biggest changes in the world. If you think you can, you're already on the right track.

MOTIVATION

July 12

"The sun himself is weak when he first rises, and gathers strength and courage as the day gets on."

Charles Dickens
19th-Century English Novelist and Social Critic

Even the sun starts out small and grows in strength. Just like the sun, you can grow stronger and braver as the day—or life—progresses.

COURAGE

July 13

"Gratitude can transform common days into thanksgivings, turn routine jobs into joy, and change ordinary opportunities into blessings."

William Arthur Ward
Motivational Writer and Columnist

Being thankful can make the mundane feel magical. Gratitude shifts your perspective, turning even the simplest things into something to celebrate.

GRATITUDE

July 14

"True friends are never apart. Maybe in distance but never in heart."

Unknown

True friendships transcend physical distance. Even when separated, the bond between true friends remains strong and unwavering.

RELATIONSHIPS

July 15

"Too often we underestimate the power of a touch, a smile, a kind word, a listening ear, or the smallest act of caring, all of which have the potential to turn a life around."

Leo Buscaglia
Author, Motivational Speaker, and Professor

Acts of kindness don't need to be grand to matter. A smile, a kind word, or a moment of understanding can change someone's day — and sometimes, their life. Even the smallest gesture can carry immeasurable love.

KINDNESS

July 16

"Education is the most powerful weapon which you can use to change the world."

Nelson Mandela

South African Anti-Apartheid Activist,
Former President of South Africa, Nobel Peace Prize Winner

Knowledge is the ultimate tool for creating change. Learning empowers you to make a real difference in the world.

WISDOM

July 17

"If you think adventure is dangerous, try routine; it's lethal."

Paulo Coelho

Brazilian Lyricist and Novelist,
Best Known for International Bestseller *The Alchemist*

Sticking to routine might feel safe, but it can drain the excitement out of life. Adventure brings life to new heights, while too much routine can dull your spirit.

WELL-BEING

July 18

"A friend is someone who knows all about you and still loves you."

Attributed to Elbert Hubbard

American Writer, Artist, and Philosopher

True friendship withstands the test of time and imperfections. It's about accepting someone for who they are, flaws and all, and offering unwavering love and support, even through life's challenges.

RELATIONSHIPS

July 19

"Sometimes, when things are falling apart, they may actually be falling into place."

J. Lynn

(Jennifer Lynn Armentrout),
Contemporary American Author

Just because everything feels like it's breaking down doesn't mean it's not leading you to something better. Trust the process, even in chaos.

COURAGE

July 20

"Whether you think you can or you think you can't, you're right."

Henry Ford

American Industrialist and
Founder of the Ford Motor Company

Your beliefs shape your reality. If you believe in yourself, you can achieve more than you think.

MOTIVATION

July 21

"Sunsets are proof that no matter what happens, every day can end beautifully."

Attributed to Kristen Butler

Author and Founder of Power of Positivity, Best Known for *3 Minute Positivity Journal*

Even on the toughest days, there's always beauty to be found. Appreciate the simple joys, find solace in nature, and remember that every day holds the promise of a fresh start.

GRATITUDE

July 22

"Love is or it ain't. Thin love ain't love at all."

Toni Morrison

Novelist and Nobel Prize Winner in Literature, Best Known for *Beloved*

Love is either genuine and unconditional, or it's not love at all. Don't settle for shallow connections or half-hearted affections. Seek relationships built on trust, respect, and deep emotional connection.

RELATIONSHIPS

July 23

"Peace cannot be kept by force; it can only be achieved by understanding."

Albert Einstein

Theoretical Physicist, Developer of the Theory of Relativity, Nobel Prize Winner in Physics

True peace cannot be achieved through force or coercion. It requires understanding, empathy, and a willingness to bridge divides through dialogue and cooperation.

KINDNESS

July 24

"Luck is what happens when preparation meets opportunity."

Seneca

(Lucius Annaeus Seneca the Younger),
Stoic Philosopher of Ancient Rome

Luck isn't random—it happens when you're ready to seize opportunities that come your way. Preparation is the key to making your own luck.

WISDOM

July 25

"Life is what happens when you're busy making other plans."

Allen Saunders

Writer, Journalist, and Cartoonist

Life is unpredictable and full of surprises. While it's important to have goals and make plans, don't get so caught up in the future that you miss out on the beautiful moments happening right now. Embrace spontaneity and be open to life's unexpected twists and turns.

WELL-BEING

July 26

> "Inaction breeds doubt and fear. Action breeds confidence and courage. If you want to conquer fear, do not sit home and think about it. Go out and get busy."

Dale Carnegie

Author and Lecturer,
Best Known for *How to Win Friends and Influence People*

Fear fades when you take action. Every small step forward builds confidence and momentum. Waiting for the perfect moment keeps you stuck — movement is what brings clarity and courage.

MOTIVATION

July 27

"You miss 100% of the shots you don't take."

Wayne Gretzky
Canadian Professional Ice Hockey Player

Taking risks and stepping outside your comfort zone is essential for growth and success. Don't let fear hold you back from pursuing your dreams and seizing opportunities.

COURAGE

July 28

"A journey is best measured in friends, rather than miles."

Tim Cahill

Travel Writer and Adventurer

The true value of a journey lies in the connections you make and the friendships you forge along the way. Cherish the people you meet and the shared experiences that create lasting bonds.

RELATIONSHIPS

July 29

"Gratitude unlocks the fullness of life. It turns what we have into enough, and more."

Melody Beattie

Author and Advocate for Healing and Recovery

Gratitude shifts your focus from what's missing to what's already here. When you appreciate the simple gifts in front of you, life expands. What once felt ordinary begins to feel abundant.

GRATITUDE

July 30

"For it is in giving that we receive."

Attributed to Francis of Assisi

Italian Mystic, Poet, and Catholic Friar who Founded the Franciscan Order

True joy comes from giving to others. The more you give, the more you gain in return.

KINDNESS

July 31

"The mind is not a vessel to be filled, but a fire to be kindled."

Plutarch

Ancient Greek Philosopher and Historian

Learning isn't just about cramming information—it's about sparking curiosity and passion. Feed your mind with ideas that light a fire within.

WISDOM

AUGUST

August 1

"Don't let someone else's opinion of you become your reality."

Les Brown
Motivational Speaker, Politician, and Author

Don't let the opinions of others define your worth or limit your potential. You are the author of your own story. Believe in yourself, trust your instincts, and create your own reality.

WELL-BEING

August 2

"The journey of a thousand miles begins with a single step."

Lao Tzu

(Laozi), Ancient Chinese Philosopher and Founder of Taoism

Even the longest and most daunting journeys begin with a single, small step. Don't be overwhelmed by the big picture; focus on taking that first step and keep moving forward, one step at a time.

MOTIVATION

August 3

"The pessimist sees difficulty in every opportunity. The optimist sees opportunity in every difficulty."

Attributed to Winston Churchill

British Prime Minister During World War II, Orator, and Statesman

Embrace a positive outlook. While pessimists focus on obstacles, optimists see potential and possibilities in every situation. Train your mind to seek solutions and opportunities, even in the face of challenges.

COURAGE

August 4

"Honesty is the first chapter in the book of wisdom."

Thomas Jefferson

3rd President of the United States, Founding Father, Best Known for the Declaration of Independence

Honesty is the foundation of a meaningful and fulfilling life. It builds trust, integrity, and authenticity, guiding your actions and decisions. Embrace honesty as a core value and strive to live in alignment with your true self.

August 5

"You can't rely on how you look to sustain you. What sustains us—what is fundamentally beautiful—is compassion, for yourself and for those around you."

Lupita Nyong'o
Kenyan-Mexican Actress, Academy Award Winner

True beauty isn't in appearances; it's in kindness and compassion. What keeps us going is love for ourselves and others.

WELL-BEING

August 6

"As much as talent counts, effort counts twice."

Angela Duckworth
Professor of Psychology, Researcher, and Author of *Grit*

Talent is important, but hard work is what makes all the difference. Effort will take you further than talent alone.

MOTIVATION

August 7

"If you can walk you can dance. If you can talk you can sing."

Zimbabwean Proverb

Everyone has the ability to find joy in simple things like dancing or singing. You don't need to be perfect—just embrace the fun of it.

COURAGE

August 8

"One's destination is never a place, but a new way of seeing things."

Henry Miller

American Novelist and Essayist

Travel and life experiences aren't just about getting to a place—they're about changing your perspective. The journey is what transforms you.

WISDOM

August 9

"He who has health, has hope; and he who has hope, has everything."

Arabic Proverb

When you're healthy, you have the strength to keep dreaming and pushing forward. Hope is the foundation for everything good in life.

WELL-BEING

August 10

"Never give up on a dream just because of the time it will take to accomplish it. The time will pass anyway."

Earl Nightingale

Radio Host, Motivational Speaker, and Author

Don't let the perceived length of a journey discourage you from pursuing your dreams. Time will pass regardless, so use it to actively work towards your goals and make your dreams a reality.

MOTIVATION

August 11

"Life is not about how fast you run or how high you climb, but how well you bounce."

Vivian Komori

American Businesswoman

Success isn't measured by speed or distance, but by how well you recover from setbacks. Resilience is the key to thriving in life.

COURAGE

August 12

"The beautiful thing about learning is nobody can take it away from you."

B.B. King

Blues Guitarist and Singer-Songwriter, Grammy Award Winner

Knowledge is something that no one can steal from you. Once you learn something, it's yours forever.

WISDOM

August 13

> "If you look at what you have in life, you'll always have more. If you look at what you don't have in life, you'll never have enough."

Oprah Winfrey
Talk Show Host, Actress, and Philanthropist

Gratitude helps you feel abundant, while focusing on what you lack leaves you feeling empty. Appreciate what you have, and more will come.

GRATITUDE

August 14

"Trust takes years to build, seconds to break, and forever to repair."

Unknown

Trust is a precious commodity that takes time and effort to build. It can be shattered in an instant, and rebuilding it can be a long and difficult process. Value trust in your relationships and strive to be trustworthy yourself.

RELATIONSHIPS

August 15

"There are three ways to ultimate success: The first way is to be kind. The second way is to be kind. The third way is to be kind."

Fred Rogers

Children's Television Host, Author, and Minister, Best Known for *Mister Rogers' Neighborhood*

Kindness is the foundation of true success. No matter what path you take, kindness will always lead you in the right direction.

KINDNESS

August 16

"All endings are also beginnings. We just don't know it at the time."

Mitch Albom

Author and Journalist,
Best Known for *Tuesdays with Morrie*

Every ending marks a new beginning. Embrace change, let go of the past, and look forward to the opportunities that lie ahead.

WISDOM

August 17

"Almost everything will work again if you unplug it for a few minutes, including you."

Anne Lamott

Novelist, Nonfiction Writer, and Writing Teacher

Sometimes the best fix is a pause. Stepping away, resting, or taking a breath can reset your energy and perspective. You're allowed to recharge.

WELL-BEING

August 18

"Love does not consist in gazing at each other, but in looking outward together in the same direction."

Antoine de Saint-Exupéry

French Writer and Aviator,
Best Known for *The Little Prince*

Love grows strongest when it's rooted in shared purpose. True connection isn't about losing yourself in another, but walking side by side—supporting each other while growing in the same direction.

RELATIONSHIPS

August 19

"Setting goals is the first step in turning the invisible into the visible."

Tony Robbins

Motivational Speaker, Life Coach, and Author

Setting clear goals gives your dreams a tangible form. It's the first step towards turning your aspirations into reality. Define what you want to achieve and create a roadmap to get there.

MOTIVATION

August 20

"Don't give in to your fears. If you do, you won't be able to talk to your heart."

Paulo Coelho

Brazilian Lyricist and Novelist,
Best Known for International Bestseller *The Alchemist*

Fear silences your true self. Don't let fear keep you from following your heart's desires.

COURAGE

August 21

"'Thank you' is the best prayer that anyone could say. I say that one a lot. 'Thank you' expresses extreme gratitude, humility, understanding."

Alice Walker

Author, Poet, Activist, and Pulitzer Prize Winner, Best Known for *The Color Purple*

Saying "thank you" is a simple but powerful way to express gratitude and humility. It's a prayer of appreciation for all the good in your life.

GRATITUDE

August 22

"Success comes when people act together; failure tends to happen alone."

Deepak Chopra

Indian-American Author, Physician, and Advocate of Mind-Body Healing

Teamwork and collaboration lead to success, while isolation often results in failure. Working with others is the key to achieving big things.

RELATIONSHIPS

August 23

"Happiness is not so much in having as sharing."

Norman MacEwan

British Royal Air Force Officer

Life is richer when we give to others, not just when we accumulate things for ourselves. True happiness comes from sharing and helping.

KINDNESS

August 24

> "Change the way you look at things and the things you look at change."

Wayne W. Dyer

Author and Motivational Speaker

Perspective is everything. When you shift how you see things, your whole world changes.

WISDOM

August 25

> "Magic is believing in yourself. If you can make that happen, you can make anything happen."

Johann Wolfgang von Goethe
18th- and 19th-Century German Writer, Poet, and Scientist

Belief in yourself is the most powerful magic. When you have confidence in your abilities, you can achieve anything you set your mind to. Embrace your potential and let your inner magic shine.

WELL-BEING

August 26

"The bad news is time flies. The good news is you're the pilot."

Michael Altshuler
Motivational Speaker and Entrepreneur

Time goes by fast, but the good news is that you're in control of how you spend it. Make the most of every moment.

MOTIVATION

August 27

> "The real voyage of discovery consists not in seeking new landscapes, but in having new eyes."

Marcel Proust

French Novelist, Best Known for *In Search of Lost Time*

True exploration isn't just about visiting new places; it's about seeing the world with fresh eyes and an open mind. Cultivate curiosity, challenge your assumptions, and discover the extraordinary in the everyday.

COURAGE

August 28

"The family is one of nature's masterpieces."

George Santayana

Spanish-American Philosopher, Essayist, and Poet

Family is one of life's purest creations — shaped by love, patience, and shared growth. When nurtured with care, it becomes a masterpiece of connection that holds us through every season of life.

RELATIONSHIPS

August 29

> "Dwell on the beauty of life. Watch the stars, and see yourself running with them."

Marcus Aurelius

2nd Century Roman Emperor and Stoic Philosopher, Best Known for *Meditations*

Take time to appreciate the beauty that surrounds you, both in the natural world and in the everyday moments of life. Find inspiration in the stars, the sunrise, or a simple act of kindness.

GRATITUDE

August 30

"The more you judge, the less you love."

Honoré de Balzac

French Novelist and Playwright of the 19th Century

The more you judge others, the less you are able to love and connect with them. Practice acceptance and compassion, recognizing that everyone is on their own unique journey.

KINDNESS

August 31

"Perception is a powerful thing. It can make us feel like we're flying on wings. Or it can bring us down, to the depths of despair, making us feel like we're going nowhere."

Itayi Garande

Author, Lawyer, and Businessman

How you see the world shapes your reality. Change your perspective, and you can lift yourself out of darkness and into light.

WISDOM

SEPTEMBER

September 1

> "Stop being afraid of getting older. With age comes wisdom and confidence."

Attributed to Robin Williams

Actor, Comedian, and Academy Award Winner

Aging is nothing to fear—it brings experience and self-assurance. Embrace it as a sign of growth, not loss.

WELL-BEING

September 2

> "Dream lofty dreams, and as you dream, so shall you become. Your vision is the promise of what you shall one day be."

James Allen

British Philosophical Writer,
Best Known for *As a Man Thinketh*

Your dreams are more than imagination — they're blueprints of who you're becoming. Every great achievement begins as a thought, a quiet vision of possibility. Nurture your dreams with belief and action, and life will rise to meet them.

MOTIVATION

September 3

"If we wait until we're ready, we'll be waiting for the rest of our lives."

Lemony Snicket

(Daniel Handler), Author,
Best Known for *A Series of Unfortunate Events*

Don't let the fear of not being fully prepared hold you back from pursuing your dreams. Take action, embrace the learning process, and allow yourself to grow and evolve along the way.

COURAGE

September 4

> "Anyone who stops learning is old, whether at twenty or eighty. Anyone who keeps learning stays young."

Henry Ford

American Industrialist and
Founder of the Ford Motor Company

Curiosity keeps the mind alive and the spirit young. Lifelong learning isn't about classrooms or textbooks; it's about staying open, curious, and eager to grow. The moment you stop learning, you stop expanding what life can be.

WISDOM

September 5

> "Once you replace negative thoughts with positive ones, you'll start having positive results."

Willie Nelson

Country Music Singer, Guitarist, Songwriter, and Grammy Award Winner

Shifting your mindset from negativity to positivity can transform your life. Focus on gratitude, optimism, and possibility, and watch as your experiences reflect this shift.

WELL-BEING

September 6

"It is a serious thing just to be alive on this fresh morning in this broken world."

Mary Oliver

American Poet, Pulitzer Prize Winner

Life itself is a gift. Even amid chaos, even when the world feels imperfect, each breath and each morning light is a reminder that presence is sacred. Gratitude begins the moment we simply notice that we are here.

GRATITUDE

September 7

> "For there is always light, if only we're brave enough to see it. If only we're brave enough to be it."

Amanda Gorman
American Poet and Activist

Even in tough times, light is there if you're willing to find it. Sometimes, you need to be the source of light for others.

COURAGE

September 8

"The power of imagination makes us infinite."

John Muir

Naturalist, Writer, Conservationist, and Advocate for Wilderness Preservation

Your imagination gives you limitless possibilities. Through creativity and dreaming, you can achieve anything.

WISDOM

September 9

> "It's your reaction to adversity, not adversity itself, that determines how your life's story will develop."

Dieter F. Uchtdorf
German Aviator and Religious Leader

It's not what happens to you but how you respond that shapes your life. You have the power to turn challenges into opportunities.

WELL-BEING

September 10

"I've failed over and over and over again in my life. And that is why I succeed."

Michael Jordan

Basketball Player and Six-Time NBA Champion

Failure is a natural part of the journey to success. Embrace your mistakes as learning opportunities and use them to fuel your growth and development. Persistence and a positive attitude will lead you to achieve your goals.

MOTIVATION

September 11

"Open the window of your mind. Allow the fresh air, new lights, and new truths to enter."

Amit Ray
Indian Author and Spiritual Teacher

Stay open to new ideas and perspectives. Letting in fresh thoughts can lead to growth and new opportunities.

COURAGE

September 12

> "Start where you are. Use what you have. Do what you can."

Arthur Ashe

Tennis Player, Activist, and Humanitarian

You don't need perfect conditions to begin. Progress starts with taking the first step, using what's already within your reach, and trusting that effort will lead the way forward.

WISDOM

September 13

"If you want to go fast, go alone. If you want to go far, go together."

African Proverb

You can accomplish more, and in a more meaningful way, when you work with others. Collaboration creates deeper success.

RELATIONSHIPS

September 14

"The happiest people don't have the best of everything, they make the best of everything."

Unknown

Happiness isn't about having it all—it's about appreciating what you've got. It's a mindset, not a material thing.

GRATITUDE

September 15

"Love is a fruit in season at all times and within reach of every hand."

Mother Teresa

Catholic Nun, Founder of the Missionaries of Charity, Nobel Peace Prize Winner

Love is always available, no matter the situation. It's something you can give and receive at any time.

KINDNESS

September 16

"You know what the happiest animal on Earth is? It's a goldfish. You know why? Got a 10-second memory. Be a goldfish."

Ted Lasso

Fictional Character from the Television Series *Ted Lasso*, Played by Jason Sudeikis

Let go of what's bothering you quickly, like a goldfish who forgets everything in seconds. Don't hold onto negativity— learn from it and move on.

WISDOM

September 17

> "When you have confidence, you can have a lot of fun. And when you have fun, you can do amazing things."

Joe Namath

American Football Player and Hall of Fame Quarterback

Confidence opens the door to enjoying life. When you're having fun, you're at your best and capable of greatness.

WELL-BEING

September 18

"If you don't build your dream, someone else will hire you to help build theirs."

Tony Gaskins
Motivational Speaker, Life Coach, and Author

If you don't pursue your own goals, you'll end up working on someone else's. It's important to invest in what you want for yourself.

MOTIVATION

September 19

> "The greatest glory in living lies not in never falling, but in rising every time we fall."

Nelson Mandela

South African Anti-Apartheid Activist,
Former President of South Africa, Nobel Peace Prize Winner

True strength isn't in never failing; it's in always getting back up after you fall. Resilience is what defines success.

COURAGE

September 20

"Walking with a friend in the dark is better than walking alone in the light."

Helen Keller

Author, Activist, and
Advocate for People with Disabilities

True friendship offers companionship, support, and understanding, even in the darkest of times. Value the friends who walk beside you through life's ups and downs.

RELATIONSHIPS

September 21

> "Anyone who keeps the ability to see beauty never grows old."

Franz Kafka

20th-Century German-Language Writer and Novelist, Best Known for *The Metamorphosis*

Staying young at heart means always seeing the beauty around you. It keeps your spirit vibrant and your days full of light.

GRATITUDE

September 22

> "Kindness is more important than wisdom, and the recognition of this is the beginning of wisdom."

Theodore Isaac Rubin
Psychiatrist and Author

True wisdom comes from understanding that kindness matters more than intelligence. Being kind is the wisest thing you can do.

KINDNESS

September 23

"One of the greatest regrets in life is being what others would want you to be, rather than being yourself."

Shannon L. Alder

Author and Therapist

Living for other people's expectations will leave you feeling empty. The real joy comes from being true to who you are, even if it's different.

WISDOM

September 24

> "Every sunset is an opportunity to reset. Every sunrise begins with new eyes."

Richie Norton

Author and Entrepreneur

Each day brings a fresh start. Endings and new beginnings both offer a chance to reset your perspective.

WELL-BEING

September 25

"'Someday' is a disease that will take your dreams to the grave with you."

Tim Ferriss

Entrepreneuer, Author, and Podcaster,
Best Known for *The 4-Hour Workweek*

Putting off your dreams for "someday" is the quickest way to never achieve them. Act now, because "someday" never comes.

MOTIVATION

September 26

> "Courage doesn't always roar. Sometimes courage is the quiet voice at the end of the day saying, 'I will try again tomorrow.'"

Mary Anne Radmacher
Writer and Artist

Being brave isn't always about big, bold actions. Sometimes, it's just about not giving up when things are tough.

COURAGE

September 27

> "Love is friendship that has caught fire. It is quiet understanding, mutual confidence, sharing and forgiving. It is loyalty through good and bad times. It settles for less than perfection and makes allowances for human weaknesses."

Ann Landers

(Esther Pauline "Eppie" Lederer), Advice Columnist

Love is rooted in friendship and grows stronger over time. It's about understanding, forgiving, and being loyal even when things aren't perfect.

RELATIONSHIPS

September 28

"Enjoy the little things, for one day you may look back and realize they were the big things."

Robert Brault

Freelance Writer and Contributor to Magazines and Newspapers

The small moments you take for granted now may end up being the ones that mean the most later. Savor the little joys in life.

GRATITUDE

September 29

> "Do your little bit of good where you are; it's those little bits of good put together that overwhelm the world."

Desmond Tutu
South African Archbishop, Anti-Apartheid and Human Rights Activist, Nobel Peace Prize Winner

Small acts of kindness add up and can make a big difference. Everyone doing a little good can change the world.

KINDNESS

September 30

"The best things in life aren't things."

Art Buchwald

American Humorist and Pulitzer Prize Winner

The most valuable parts of life aren't objects—they're experiences, relationships, and moments of joy.

WISDOM

OCTOBER

October 1

> "There is no Wi-Fi in the forest, but I promise you will find a better connection."

Ralph Smart
British Psychologist, Author, and Life Coach

Being in nature disconnects you from technology but reconnects you with yourself. It's the best kind of connection.

WELL-BEING

October 2

> "You're off to Great Places! Today is your day! Your mountain is waiting, So... get on your way!"

Dr. Seuss

(Theodor Seuss Geisel),
American Children's Author and Illustrator

Today is your day to shine! Embrace the challenges and opportunities that lie ahead, and embark on your journey with confidence and excitement.

MOTIVATION

October 3

"We don't even know how strong we are until we are forced to bring that hidden strength forward."

Isabel Allende

Chilean-American Author,
Best Known for *The House of the Spirits*

Sometimes you don't realize how strong you are until life forces you to dig deep. Tough times reveal your true strength.

COURAGE

October 4

> "Sometimes the most important thing in a whole day is the rest we take between two deep breaths."

Etty Hillesum

Dutch Jewish Diarist and Holocaust Victim

Wisdom isn't always found in big decisions. Sometimes it lives in the pauses, in the quiet moments that remind us to be fully here, to breathe, and to begin again.

WISDOM

October 5

"Instead of worrying about what you cannot control, shift your energy to what you can create."

Roy T. Bennett
Author, Best Known for *The Light in the Heart*

Focus your energy on what you can influence and create, rather than dwelling on things beyond your control. This empowers you to take action and shape your own reality.

WELL-BEING

October 6

"Nothing is impossible. The word itself says 'I'm possible!'"

Audrey Hepburn

British Actress and Humanitarian

Believe in the power of possibility. Nothing is truly impossible if you set your mind to it and act. Embrace challenges, overcome obstacles, and strive to achieve your dreams, no matter how big or audacious they may seem.

MOTIVATION

October 7

"The secret of happiness is freedom, and the secret of freedom is courage."

Thucydides
Ancient Greek Historian and General, 5th Century BCE

Happiness comes from being free to live authentically. Freedom requires courage to step out of your comfort zone and be true to yourself.

COURAGE

October 8

"Let yourself be silently drawn by the strange pull of what you really love. It will not lead you astray."

Rumi

(Jalal al-Din Rumi), Persian Poet and
Sufi Mystic of the 13th Century

Follow your passions and let them guide you on your journey. Trust your instincts and pursue what truly excites and inspires you, and you'll find your path to fulfillment.

WISDOM

October 9

"Adopt the pace of nature: her secret is patience."

Ralph Waldo Emerson

Essayist, Poet, Philosopher, and
Leader of the Transcendentalist Movement

Embrace the natural flow of life, just like nature does. True growth and wisdom come with patience and allowing things to unfold in their own time.

WELL-BEING

October 10

"If my mind can conceive it, and my heart can believe it, then I can achieve it."

Jesse Jackson

Civil Rights Activist, Politician, and Minister

If you can dream something and truly believe in it, you have the power to make it a reality. Your mind and heart are the keys to achieving great things.

MOTIVATION

October 11

> "Courage is not having the strength to go on; it is going on when you don't have the strength."

Attributed to Theodore Roosevelt
26th President of the United States, Writer, and Naturalist

Courage is pushing forward even when you feel like you can't. It's about finding the will to keep going, even when it's hard.

COURAGE

October 12

"In the end, it's not the years in your life that count. It's the life in your years."

Edward J. Stieglitz

Physician and Author,
Best Known for *The Second Forty Years*

It's not about how long you live but how much life you put into your years.
Make every moment count.

WISDOM

October 13

> "The most beautiful discovery true friends make is that they can grow separately without growing apart."

Elisabeth Foley

American Writer

The most beautiful aspect of true friendship is the ability to support each other's growth and evolution, even as you pursue different paths in life. Celebrate each other's successes and remain connected through shared values and love.

RELATIONSHIPS

October 14

"In a world where you can be anything, be kind."

Unknown

Of all the qualities you can choose to embody, kindness is the most important. It makes the world better for everyone.

KINDNESS

October 15

> "The root of joy is gratefulness... It is not joy that makes us grateful; it is gratitude that makes us joyful."

David Steindl-Rast

Benedictine Monk, Author, and Teacher of Grateful Living

Joy begins with gratitude. When you pause to appreciate what already surrounds you, contentment naturally follows. Gratitude shifts your focus from what's missing to the quiet abundance already in your life.

GRATITUDE

October 16

"Those who wish to sing always find a song."

Swedish Proverb

If you have the desire to find joy, you'll always find a reason to be happy. It's all about your mindset.

WELL-BEING

October 17

"All things are difficult before they are easy."

Thomas Fuller
17th-Century English Clergyman and Historian

Every challenge feels hard at first, but with time and effort, it gets easier. Don't give up just because it's tough in the beginning.

MOTIVATION

October 18

"The only place success comes before work is in the dictionary."

Vince Lombardi

American Football Coach and Executive

Success doesn't just happen on its own—it takes effort and dedication. Hard work is always the foundation for achieving anything meaningful.

WISDOM

October 19

"Be yourself; everyone else is already taken."

Attributed to Oscar Wilde

Irish Poet and Playwright

Embrace your unique qualities and express your true self authentically. Don't try to fit into a mold or compare yourself to others; celebrate your individuality and let your light shine.

COURAGE

October 20

"Being deeply loved by someone gives you strength, while loving someone deeply gives you courage."

Attributed to Lao Tzu

(Laozi), Ancient Chinese Philosopher and Founder of Taoism

Love from others makes you feel strong, but loving others gives you the courage to face anything. It's a two-way street that builds resilience.

RELATIONSHIPS

October 21

"Everyone you meet is fighting a battle you know nothing about. Be kind. Always."

Robin Williams

Actor, Comedian, and Academy Award Winner

Everyone is going through something difficult, even if you don't see it. Kindness is important because you never know what someone is dealing with.

KINDNESS

October 22

"The present moment is filled with joy and happiness. If you are attentive, you will see it."

Thích Nhất Hạnh

Vietnamese Buddhist Monk, Poet, and Peace Activist

Happiness is all around you in the present moment if you take the time to notice it. Mindfulness opens your eyes to the joy in everyday life.

GRATITUDE

October 23

"The body is precious. It is our vehicle for awakening. Treat it with care."

Attributed to the Buddha

(Sidhartha Gautama),
Religious Teacher and Founder of Buddhism

Your body is a gift that allows you to experience life. Taking care of it is essential for living fully.

WELL-BEING

October 24

"Your future is created by what you do today, not tomorrow."

Robert Kiyosaki

Businessman and Author,
Best Known for *Rich Dad Poor Dad*

What you do right now shapes the life you're going to have. Don't wait—start building your future today.

MOTIVATION

October 25

"Every child is an artist. The problem is how to remain an artist once we grow up."

Pablo Picasso

Spanish Artist of the 20th Century and Co-Founder of Cubism

We're all born with a creative spark. Don't let the pressures of adulthood extinguish it. Nurture your artistic spirit, embrace your passions, and continue to express yourself through art, music, or any form of creativity that brings you joy.

WISDOM

October 26

"A person who never made a mistake never tried anything new."

Albert Einstein

Theoretical Physicist, Developer of the Theory of Relativity, Nobel Prize Winner in Physics

Mistakes are part of trying new things and growing. If you're not making mistakes, you're not stepping outside your comfort zone.

COURAGE

October 27

"Loving and energizing others is the best possible thing we can do for ourselves."

James Redfield

Writer, Screenwriter, and Film Producer,
Best Known for *The Celestine Prophecy*

By uplifting and supporting others, you not only make a positive impact on their lives but also cultivate your own happiness and sense of fulfillment.

RELATIONSHIPS

October 28

> "Let us be grateful to the people who make us happy; they are the charming gardeners who make our souls blossom."

Marcel Proust

French Novelist, Best Known for *In Search of Lost Time*

Express gratitude for the people who bring joy and happiness into your life. They nurture your spirit and help you blossom into your best self.

GRATITUDE

October 29

"Nobody deserves your tears, but whoever deserves them will not make you cry."

Gabriel García Márquez

Colombian Novelist and Nobel Prize Winner in Literature, Best Known for *One Hundred Years of Solitude*

The people truly worth your love won't bring you pain. Those who care about you will treat you with kindness, not cause tears.

KINDNESS

October 30

"Forgive others not because they deserve forgiveness, but because you deserve peace."

Jonathan Lockwood Huie
Author of Books on Self-Awareness and Personal Growth

Forgiveness is a gift you give yourself. It allows you to let go of the past, heal emotional wounds, and move forward with a lighter heart. Choose forgiveness and reclaim your inner peace.

WELL-BEING

October 31

"You can make anything by writing."

C.S. Lewis

British Writer, Scholar, and Theologian, Best Known for *The Chronicles of Narnia*

Writing is a powerful tool for self-expression, creativity, and communication. Whether it's journaling, storytelling, or crafting poetry, use writing to explore your thoughts, share your ideas, and bring your imagination to life.

MOTIVATION

NOVEMBER

November 1

"The way to cope with the future is to create it."

Ilya Prigogine

Belgian Physical Chemist,
Nobel Prize Winner in Chemistry

The future isn't something that just happens to you; it's something you actively shape through your choices and actions today. Take charge of your life and create the future you desire.

COURAGE

November 2

"Being vulnerable is a strength, not a weakness."

Selena Gomez

Singer, Actress, and Advocate

Letting yourself be open and honest is a sign of courage, not weakness. Vulnerability allows for deeper connections and growth.

WISDOM

November 3

"The greatest wealth is health."

Attributed to Virgil

Ancient Roman Poet of the 1st Century BCE,
Best Known for *The Aeneid*

Good health is the most valuable asset you possess. Prioritize your physical and mental well-being through healthy habits, exercise, and self-care. A healthy body and mind are the foundation for a fulfilling life.

WELL-BEING

November 4

"The world is but a canvas to the imagination."

Henry David Thoreau

19th-Century American Transcendentalist Writer, Philosopher, and Naturalist

The world is full of possibilities, limited only by how far your imagination can stretch. Be creative with how you view and experience life.

MOTIVATION

November 5

> "Darkness cannot drive out darkness; only light can do that. Hate cannot drive out hate; only love can do that."

Martin Luther King Jr.

Baptist Minister, Civil Rights Leader, and Nobel Peace Prize Winner

Darkness and hate can only be overcome with light and love. Choose compassion over anger, understanding over prejudice, and kindness over cruelty. Be a beacon of positivity and contribute to a more loving and harmonious world.

KINDNESS

November 6

"Love is like the wind, you can't see it but you can feel it."

Nicholas Sparks

Novelist and Screenwriter, Best Known for *The Notebook*

Love isn't something you always notice with your eyes, but you'll feel it deeply. It's invisible, but its presence is undeniable.

WISDOM

November 7

> "Dance is the hidden language of the soul of the body."

Martha Graham
Modern Dancer and Choreographer

Dance expresses emotions and feelings that words cannot. It connects the body and soul, revealing inner truths through movement.

WELL-BEING

November 8

"My mission in life is not merely to survive, but to thrive; and to do so with some passion, some compassion, some humor, and some style."

Maya Angelou

American Poet, Author, and Civil Rights Activist

You're here to do more than simply exist. Live boldly, love deeply, laugh often, and let your unique spark shine through.

MOTIVATION

November 9

"In order for the light to shine so brightly, the darkness must be present."

Francis Bacon

16th–17th Century Philosopher, Scientist, and Advocate for Scientific Inquiry

You appreciate the good times more because you've experienced tough ones. Darkness helps highlight the beauty of the light.

COURAGE

November 10

"Happiness resides not in possessions, and not in gold, happiness dwells in the soul."

Democritus
Ancient Greek Philosopher of the 5th Century BCE

Happiness doesn't come from owning things or having money. True happiness comes from within you—your feelings, thoughts, and how you live your life.

WISDOM

November 11

"Laughter is the sound of the soul dancing."

Jarod Kintz
Self-Published Author and Humorist

Laughter is an expression of pure joy and a reflection of your inner spirit. Embrace laughter as a way to connect with others, celebrate life's moments, and nourish your soul.

WELL-BEING

November 12

"I believe that if you'll just stand up and go, life will open up for you."

Tina Turner

Singer, Songwriter, and Grammy Award Winner, Best Known as the "Queen of Rock 'n' Roll"

Sometimes all it takes is the courage to start. Once you take that step, opportunities begin to appear.

MOTIVATION

November 13

> "The more I traveled, the more I realized that fear makes strangers of people who should be friends."

Shirley MacLaine

Actress, Author, and Academy Award Winner

Fear creates barriers and divides us from others. Travel and experiencing different cultures can break down those barriers, fostering understanding and connection between people from all walks of life.

RELATIONSHIPS

November 14

"Gratitude is one of the most powerful human emotions. Once expressed, it changes attitude, brightens outlook, and broadens our perspective."

Germany Kent
Journalist, Producer, and Author

When you practice gratitude, you shift from focusing on what you don't have to appreciating what you do. This mindset attracts even more positivity into your life.

GRATITUDE

November 15

"If you want help, help others. If you want love, give it. If you want respect, show it. Whatever you want more of, start giving more of."

Unknown

Whatever you're seeking from the world, start by giving it to others. The energy you put out is what you'll get back.

KINDNESS

November 16

> "You can't change what's going on around you until you start changing what's going on within you."

Zig Ziglar
Author, Salesman, and Motivational Speaker

Real change starts from within. Work on your mindset and your attitude, and the rest will follow.

WELL-BEING

November 17

"We are not what we know but what we are willing to learn."

Mary Catherine Bateson

Cultural Anthropologist and Writer

What defines you isn't what you already know, but your openness to new learning. Growth comes from the willingness to explore the unknown.

MOTIVATION

November 18

"Have the courage to live a life true to yourself, not the life others expect of you."

Bronnie Ware

Australian Author, Songwriter, and Motivational Speaker, Best Known for *The Top Five Regrets of the Dying*

Don't waste time living for other people's approval. Be bold enough to follow your own path and live authentically.

COURAGE

November 19

"Life can only be understood backwards; but it must be lived forwards."

Søren Kierkegaard

Danish Theologian and Existentialist Philosopher

You can only make sense of life by looking back, but you have to keep moving forward. Learn from the past, but don't dwell there.

WISDOM

November 20

"Connection gives purpose and meaning to our lives."

Brené Brown

Research Professor, Author, and Podcast Host,
Best Known for Her Work on Vulnerability

Meaningful connections with others give our lives purpose and direction. Cultivate relationships built on trust, respect, and shared values. These connections will enrich your life and provide support during challenging times.

RELATIONSHIPS

November 21

> "I have found that if you love life, life will love you back."

Arthur Rubinstein

20th Century Polish-American Classical Pianist, Grammy Lifetime Achievement Award Winner

If you approach life with excitement and positivity, it will reward you with more of the same. Your attitude toward life shapes how life treats you.

GRATITUDE

November 22

"Be the change that you wish to see in the world."

Attributed to Mahatma Gandhi

Leading Figure of the Indian Independence Movement, Advocate for Nonviolent Resistance

Instead of waiting for others to act, take initiative and lead by example. Your actions, no matter how small, can inspire others and create a positive impact.

KINDNESS

November 23

"It's not about having enough time, it's about making enough time."

Rachael Bermingham

Australian Author, Entrepreneur, and Motivational Speaker

It's not about having endless hours, but about prioritizing what truly matters and making time for the things that bring you joy and fulfillment.

WELL-BEING

November 24

"The most effective way to do it, is to do it."

Amelia Earhart

American Aviator, Record-Setting Pilot, and Advocate for Women in Aviation

The best way to accomplish something is simply to get started. Action is what makes things happen.

MOTIVATION

November 25

"Doubt kills more dreams than failure ever will."

Suzy Kassem

Writer, Poet, and Philosopher

Self-doubt can be a powerful obstacle to achieving your dreams. Don't let fear or uncertainty hold you back. Believe in yourself, overcome your doubts, and take bold action towards your goals.

COURAGE

November 26

"You don't become what you want, you become what you believe."

Oprah Winfrey

Talk Show Host, Actress, and Philanthropist

Your core beliefs shape your reality more than your passing thoughts or desires. Believe in yourself, and you'll become who you're meant to be.

WISDOM

November 27

> "The most precious gift we can offer others is our presence. When our mindfulness embraces those we love, they will bloom like flowers."

Thích Nhất Hạnh
Vietnamese Buddhist Monk, Poet, and Peace Activist

Being fully present with the people you care about is the greatest gift you can give. Your attention helps others grow and thrive.

RELATIONSHIPS

November 28

"Gratitude is not only the greatest of virtues, but the parent of all the others."

Cicero

Roman Statesman, Philosopher, and Orator of the 1st Century BCE

Gratitude is the cornerstone of a fulfilling life. It cultivates other positive qualities like generosity, compassion, and humility. By appreciating the good in your life, you open your heart to abundance and create a positive influence around you.

GRATITUDE

November 29

"Let us always meet each other with a smile, for the smile is the beginning of love."

Mother Teresa

Catholic Nun, Founder of the Missionaries of Charity, Nobel Peace Prize Winner

A smile is a simple yet powerful gesture that can bridge gaps and foster connection. Greet others with warmth and kindness, and watch as love and positivity blossom.

KINDNESS

November 30

> "Life is tough, darling. Life is hard. And we better laugh at everything, otherwise we're going down the tube."

Joan Rivers

Comedian, Actress, Writer, and Talk Show Host

Life can be difficult, but humor helps you get through the challenges. Laughing keeps your spirit light when things feel heavy.

WELL-BEING

DECEMBER

December 1

"Real change, enduring change, happens one step at a time."

Ruth Bader Ginsburg

Lawyer and Former Associate Justice of the U.S. Supreme Court, Advocate for Gender Equality

Big changes don't happen overnight—they come from small, consistent steps. Take it one day at a time and trust the process.

MOTIVATION

December 2

"If you think you're too small to make a difference, try sleeping with a mosquito."

African Proverb

Even the smallest actions can make a difference. Don't underestimate your own power to create positive change in the world. Every act of kindness, every voice raised for justice, every effort to make the world a better place matters.

WISDOM

December 3

"Nobody who ever gave his best regretted it."

George Halas

American Football Player, Coach, and Founder of the Chicago Bears

When you give something your all, even if you don't win, you'll feel good about the effort. There's no room for regrets when you've done your best.

COURAGE

December 4

"In a way, you've already won in this world because you're the only one who can be you."

Fred Rogers

Children's Television Host, Author, and Minister, Best Known for *Mister Rogers' Neighborhood*

You're already unique, and that's your superpower. No one else can be you, and that's something to celebrate.

WELL-BEING

December 5

"Be not afraid of growing slowly; be afraid only of standing still."

Chinese Proverb

Progress, even if it's slow, is still progress. What you should fear is not moving at all.

MOTIVATION

December 6

"Tenderness and kindness are not signs of weakness and despair, but manifestations of strength and resolution."

Kahlil Gibran

Lebanese-American Writer, Poet, and Artist

Being kind and tender-hearted isn't weak—it takes strength and courage to show softness in a tough world.

KINDNESS

December 7

"Age is no barrier. It's a limitation you put on your mind."

Jackie Joyner-Kersee
American Track and Field Athlete and Six-Time Olympic Medalist

Don't let societal expectations or self-imposed limitations hold you back from pursuing your passions and living life to the fullest. Embrace your age, embrace your experiences, and continue to learn and grow.

COURAGE

December 8

> "Some old-fashioned things like fresh air and sunshine are hard to beat."

Laura Ingalls Wilder
American Writer and Teacher,
Best Known for *Little House on the Prairie*

Simple pleasures like being outside in the fresh air are timeless. Nature's gifts never get old.

WELL-BEING

December 9

> "Dreams are the seeds of change. Nothing ever grows without a seed, and nothing ever changes without a dream."

Debby Boone
Singer, Songwriter, and Grammy Award Winner

Dreams are the catalysts for transformation and progress. Nurture your dreams, believe in their power, and take action to turn them into reality. Without dreams, there can be no growth or positive change in the world.

MOTIVATION

December 10

"Gratitude is one of the strongest and most transformative states of being. It shifts your perspective from lack to abundance and allows you to focus on the good in your life, which in turn pulls more goodness into your reality."

Jen Sincero
Author, Motivational Speaker, and Success Coach

Gratitude changes the way you see the world. By focusing on what you're thankful for, you invite even more good things into your life.

GRATITUDE

December 11

"Love doesn't just sit there, like a stone; it has to be made, like bread; remade all the time, made new."

Ursula K. Le Guin

Author, Best Known for her Works of Science Fiction

Love requires effort and attention to keep it alive. It's something you have to nurture and renew every day.

RELATIONSHIPS

December 12

"All you need is love. But a little chocolate now and then doesn't hurt."

Charles M. Schulz

American Cartoonist,
Best Known for Comic Strip *Peanuts*

Love is essential to life, but it's okay to enjoy simple pleasures like chocolate along the way. A reminder to mix in joy and indulgence with the serious stuff.

WISDOM

December 13

"Whatever you are, be a good one."

William Makepeace Thackeray

19th-Century English Novelist,
Best Known for *Vanity Fair*

Strive for excellence in whatever you do. Whether it's your studies, your hobbies, or your relationships, commit to being the best version of yourself.

MOTIVATION

December 14

"Your time is limited, don't waste it living someone else's life."

Steve Jobs

Entrepreneur, Inventor, and Investor,
Co-Founder of Apple

Your time on this earth is precious and finite. Don't waste it trying to live up to someone else's expectations or following a path that doesn't resonate with your true self. Live authentically and make choices that align with your values and dreams.

COURAGE

December 15

"As you grow older, you will discover that you have two hands — one for helping yourself, the other for helping others."

Sam Levenson
Humorist, Author, and Television Host

We each hold the power to shape our own path and to lift others along the way. Life calls for both hands, one to build and one to give. Kindness is not passive; it is how we take part in creating a better world.

KINDNESS

December 16

> "Grief, I've learned, is really just love. It's all the love you want to give but cannot. All that unspent love gathers up in the corners of your eyes, the lump in your throat, and in that hollow part of your chest. Grief is just love with no place to go."

Jamie Anderson

Writer and Poet

Grief is the love we feel when we lose someone. It's all the love we still have but no longer have a place to send.

RELATIONSHIPS

December 17

"Sometimes when you're in a dark place you think you've been buried but you've actually been planted."

Christine Caine
Australian Activist, Author, and Speaker

Tough times can feel like the end, but they're often the start of something new. You're not buried—you're growing.

WELL-BEING

December 18

"The future belongs to those who believe in the beauty of their dreams."

Eleanor Roosevelt

First Lady of the United States and Human Rights Activist

The future belongs to those who dare to dream big and believe in the power of their aspirations. Cultivate a positive mindset, visualize your goals, and take consistent action to manifest your dreams into reality.

COURAGE

December 19

"Stay close to anything that makes you glad you are alive."

Attributed to Hafez
Persian Lyric Poet of the 14th Century

Surround yourself with people, activities, and places that make you feel happy to be alive. Life's too short to spend time on things that don't bring joy.

GRATITUDE

December 20

"One day spent with someone you love can change everything."

Mitch Albom

Author and Journalist,
Best Known for *Tuesdays with Morrie*

Spending quality time with loved ones can create profound and lasting memories. Cherish those moments, express your love, and nurture the relationships that matter most.

RELATIONSHIPS

December 21

"A good laugh and a long sleep are the best cures in the doctor's book."

Irish proverb

Sometimes, all you need to feel better is a laugh and a good night's rest. These simple things can reset your body and your mind.

WELL-BEING

December 22

"Courage starts with showing up and letting ourselves be seen."

Brené Brown

Research Professor, Author, and Podcast Host,
Best Known for Her Work on Vulnerability

Courage begins with showing up authentically and allowing yourself to be vulnerable. Embrace your true self, share your thoughts and feelings, and don't be afraid to let others see your imperfections.

COURAGE

December 23

> "Mistakes are a fact of life. It is the response to the error that counts."

Nikki Giovanni
Poet, Writer, Activist, and Educator

Mistakes are part of the learning process. What truly matters is how you respond—by learning, taking responsibility, and growing from them.

WISDOM

December 24

"The weak can never forgive. Forgiveness is the attribute of the strong."

Mahatma Gandhi

Leading Figure of the Indian Independence Movement, Advocate for Nonviolent Resistance

Forgiveness is a sign of strength, not weakness. Holding onto anger and resentment only hurts you. Choose to forgive those who have wronged you, not because they deserve it, but because you deserve peace and freedom from negativity.

KINDNESS

December 25

> "The more you praise and celebrate your life, the more there is in life to celebrate."

Oprah Winfrey
Talk Show Host, Actress, and Philanthropist

Focusing on the positive and showing gratitude attracts more joy. Celebrating life creates a cycle of happiness.

GRATITUDE

December 26

> "One of the lessons that I grew up with was to always stay true to yourself and never let what somebody else says distract you from your goals."

Michelle Obama

Attorney and Former First Lady of the United States, Advocate for Education and Health

Stay focused on your own path and don't let the opinions of others throw you off. Staying true to yourself is the key to success.

MOTIVATION

December 27

"Friendship is born at that moment when one person says to another, 'What! You too? I thought I was the only one.'"

C.S. Lewis

British Writer, Scholar, and Theologian, Best Known for *The Chronicles of Narnia*

True friendships often start when you realize you're not alone in your thoughts or experiences. It's that moment of connection over shared understanding.

RELATIONSHIPS

December 28

"You are searching the world for treasure, but the real treasure is yourself."

Rumi

(Jalal al-Din Rumi), Persian Poet and
Sufi Mystic of the 13th Century

We spend so much time looking for things outside of us to make us happy, but the real prize is who you already are. Your worth and potential are the greatest treasure you'll ever find.

WELL-BEING

December 29

"Spread love wherever you go. Let no one ever come to you without leaving happier."

Mother Teresa

Catholic Nun, Founder of the Missionaries of Charity, Nobel Peace Prize Winner

Be a source of love and positivity for everyone you meet. Even small acts of kindness can brighten someone's day.

KINDNESS

December 30

"A dead end is just a good place to turn around."

Naomi Judd

Country Music Singer, Songwriter, Actress, and Grammy Award Winner

Hitting a wall doesn't mean it's over—it's just a signal to take a new path. There's always a way forward, even if it means turning around.

WISDOM

December 31

"Wherever you go, go with all your heart."

Confucius
Chinese Philosopher and Teacher,
Founder of Confucianism, 6th–5th Centuries BCE

Wherever life takes you, approach it with passion, enthusiasm, and wholehearted commitment. Give your best effort in everything you do and embrace the journey with an open and engaged heart.

COURAGE

A Life of Sparks

As you come to the end of this book, I want to take a moment with you. We have moved through 366 days together, page by page, spark by spark. I hope these words have offered more than just inspiration. I hope they have felt like quiet moments of connection. I hope they reminded you to pause, to reflect, to take a breath, and to return to what matters most.

When I first began collecting these quotes, my heart was focused on my daughters. I wanted them to have something they could turn to. A reminder that they are never alone. That wisdom is everywhere. That even on the hardest days, they can still choose joy. Over time, I realized this book was not just for them. It was for anyone who might find themselves searching for clarity, for comfort, or for courage.

Life is unpredictable. It will challenge you in ways you never expect. It will surprise you, stretch you, and sometimes slow you down. In those moments, I hope you remember that even the smallest spark can light your way forward. I hope you continue to notice the power of kindness, the quiet strength of showing up, and the wisdom that lives in everyday life.

My wish is that this book becomes something you return to. Not just when you are struggling, but when you are celebrating. When you want to feel grounded. When you are ready to grow. These sparks were meant to travel. Let them live in your journals, your conversations, your choices, and your dreams.

Daily Spark began as a family gift, created with love for my daughters, and it has slowly evolved into something more. Thank you for making it part of your own story. Thank you for reading with an open heart. May you continue to live with intention, joy, and love. And may each spark you carry forward help light the path for someone else.

— Sara

To my daughters, and to everyone who finds these pages: may you always remember that the smallest spark can light the way. Carry kindness, courage, and gratitude into each day, and trust that you already have what it takes to make your life the best it can be.

— Giovanni

www.ingramcontent.com/pod-product-compliance
Lightning Source LLC
Chambersburg PA
CBHW030451100526
44580CB00006B/87/J